ASCENT
CENTER FOR TECHNICAL KNOWLEDGE

Autodesk® Revit® 2017 (R1)
Architecture: Site and Structural Design

Student Guide
Imperial - 1st Edition

AUTODESK.
Authorized Publisher

ASCENT - Center for Technical Knowledge®
Autodesk® Revit® 2017 (R1)
Architecture: Site and Structural Design
Imperial - 1st Edition

Prepared and produced by:

ASCENT Center for Technical Knowledge
630 Peter Jefferson Parkway, Suite 175
Charlottesville, VA 22911

866-527-2368
www.ASCENTed.com

Lead Contributor: Martha Hollowell

ASCENT - Center for Technical Knowledge is a division of Rand Worldwide, Inc., providing custom developed knowledge products and services for leading engineering software applications. ASCENT is focused on specializing in the creation of education programs that incorporate the best of classroom learning and technology-based training offerings.

We welcome any comments you may have regarding this student guide, or any of our products. To contact us please email: feedback@ASCENTed.com.

AS-RAR1701-SSD1IM-SG   //   IS-RAR1701-SSD1IM-SG

Contents

Preface

The main purpose of the Autodesk® Revit® Architecture software is to design buildings: walls, doors, floors, roofs, and stairs. However, architects also frequently need to add site and structural information. The *Autodesk® Revit® 2017 (R1) Architecture: Site and Structural Design* student guide covers the elements and tools that are used to create topographic surfaces for site work and add structural elements.

Site Topics Covered

- Create topographic surfaces

- Add property lines and building pads

- Modify toposurfaces with subregions, splitting surfaces and grading the regions

- Annotate site plans and add site components

- Work with Shared Coordinates

Structural Topics Covered

- Create structural grids and add columns

- Add foundation walls and footings

- Add beams and beam systems

- Create framing elevations and add braces

Note on Software Setup

This student guide assumes a standard installation of the software using the default preferences during installation. Lectures and practices use the standard software templates and default options for the Content Libraries.

Students and Educators can Access Free Autodesk Software and Resources

Autodesk challenges you to get started with free educational licenses for professional software and creativity apps used by millions of architects, engineers, designers, and hobbyists today. Bring Autodesk software into your classroom, studio, or workshop to learn, teach, and explore real-world design challenges the way professionals do.

Get started today - register at the Autodesk Education Community and download one of the many Autodesk software applications available.

Visit www.autodesk.com/joinedu/

Note: Free products are subject to the terms and conditions of the end-user license and services agreement that accompanies the software. The software is for personal use for education purposes and is not intended for classroom or lab use.

Lead Contributor: Martha Hollowell

Martha incorporates her passion for architecture and education into all her projects, including the training guides she creates on Autodesk Revit for Architecture, MEP, and Structure. She started working with AutoCAD in the early 1990's, adding AutoCAD Architecture and Autodesk Revit as they came along.

After receiving a B.Sc. in Architecture from the University of Virginia, she worked in the architectural department of the Colonial Williamsburg Foundation and later in private practice, consulting with firms setting up AutoCAD in their offices.

Martha has over 20 years' experience as a trainer and instructional designer. She is skilled in leading individuals and small groups to understand and build on their potential. Martha is trained in Instructional Design and has achieved the Autodesk Certified Instructor (ACI) and Autodesk Certified Professional designations for Revit Architecture.

Martha Hollowell has been the Lead Contributor for *Autodesk Revit Architecture: Site and Structural Design* since its initial release in 2008.

In this Guide

The following images highlight some of the features that can be found in this Student Guide.

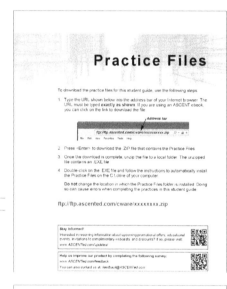

FTP link for practice files

Practice Files

The Practice Files page tells you how to download and install the practice files that are provided with this student guide.

Learning Objectives for the chapter

Chapters

Each chapter begins with a brief introduction and a list of the chapter's Learning Objectives.

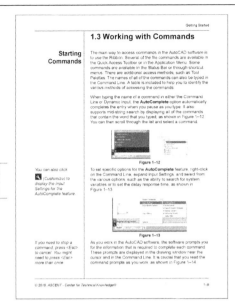

Instructional Content

Each chapter is split into a series of sections of instructional content on specific topics. These lectures include the descriptions, step-by-step procedures, figures, hints, and information you need to achieve the chapter's Learning Objectives.

Side notes

Side notes are hints or additional information for the current topic.

Practice Objectives

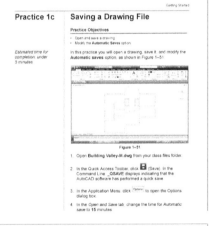

Practices

Practices enable you to use the software to perform a hands-on review of a topic.

Some practices require you to use prepared practice files, which can be downloaded from the link found on the Practice Files page.

Chapter Review Questions

Chapter review questions, located at the end of each chapter, enable you to review the key concepts and learning objectives of the chapter.

Command Summary

The Command Summary is located at the end of each chapter. It contains a list of the software commands that are used throughout the chapter, and provides information on where the command is found in the software.

Autodesk Certification Exam Appendix

This appendix includes a list of the topics and objectives for the Autodesk Certification exams, and the chapter and section in which the relevant content can be found.

Icons in this Student Guide

The following icons are used to help you quickly and easily find helpful information.

Indicates items that are new in the Autodesk Revit 2017 (R1) software.

Indicates items that have been enhanced in the Autodesk Revit 2017 (R1) software.

Practice Files

To download the practice files for this student guide, use the following steps:

1. Type the URL shown below into the address bar of your Internet browser. The URL must be typed **exactly as shown**. If you are using an ASCENT ebook, you can click on the link to download the file.

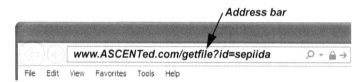

Address bar

www.ASCENTed.com/getfile?id=sepiida

File   Edit   View   Favorites   Tools   Help

2. Press <Enter> to download the .ZIP file that contains the Practice Files.

3. Once the download is complete, unzip the file to a local folder. The unzipped file contains an .EXE file.

4. Double-click on the .EXE file and follow the instructions to automatically install the Practice Files on the C:\ drive of your computer.

   Do not change the location in which the Practice Files folder is installed. Doing so can cause errors when completing the practices in this student guide.

http://www.ASCENTed.com/getfile?id=sepiida

Stay Informed!

Interested in receiving information about upcoming promotional offers, educational events, invitations to complimentary webcasts, and discounts? If so, please visit:

www.ASCENTed.com/updates/

Help us improve our product by completing the following survey:

www.ASCENTed.com/feedback

You can also contact us at: *feedback@ASCENTed.com*

Site Design

The design aspect of placing a building on a site is a thoughtful process. It helps to be able to try out different locations. To do this within the Autodesk® Revit® software, you can create and make basic modifications to toposurfaces. These toposurfaces can be sketched directly in the project, or linked into the project using a CAD file or points file provided by the surveyor or civil engineer. Once you have a toposurface in place, you can add property lines, cut out space for a building pad, and even create grading for a surface. Toposurfaces can support components, such as parking spaces and trees.

Learning Objectives in this Chapter

- Set the Project Base Point and Survey Point.
- Create toposurfaces.
- Create property lines.
- Create building pads within a toposurface.
- Create subregions of a toposurface.
- Split and join the surfaces of a toposurface.
- Grade toposurfaces.
- Annotate toposurfaces.
- Add site and parking components to toposurfaces.
- Publish and acquire coordinates between host and linked models.

1.1 Preparing a Project for Site Design

The foundation of site elements is the topography or surface structure, which is displayed with contours that connect points of equal heights. To place a project model correctly on a toposurface, there is underlying information that you need. You should set the Project Base Point and Survey Point (as shown in Figure 1–1) early in the project because they impact the exact coordinates, elevation, and True North angle of the project. If you are using a linked file that contains information such as the survey point, you can acquire that point from the linked file.

This figure is shown at Project North. If it was at True North, the building and site would be angled and the Survey Point would be straight.

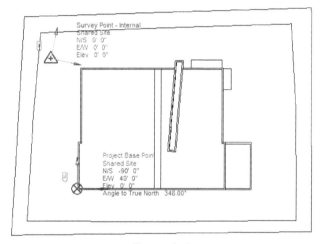

Figure 1–1

- Every project has a Project Base Point (0,0,0) and a Survey Point. These points can be at the same location, causing the icons to overlap.

- The icons typically display in site plan views. To display them in other views, in the Visibility Graphics dialog box, in the *Model Categories* tab, expand *Site* and select **Project Base Point** and **Survey Point**.

Survey Point

The Survey Point is a specific point in the physical environment, such as a survey marker. You can specify the Survey Point coordinates directly, or you can acquire this survey point from a linked file (such as a .DWG) from which the topography information is gathered.

- To change the internal Survey Point, unclip it (🔖), and then change the information in the Survey Point or in Properties.

Project Base Point

The Project Base Point defines the origin of the project coordinate system, which is the 0,0,0 point of the building model. It is helpful to have the Project Base Point at a useful place in the project (such as the intersection of principle grid lines or the corner of the building), as shown in Figure 1–2.

To modify the Project Base Point, click on the icon and modify *N/S*, *E/W*, *Elev*, and *Angle to True North* as required, or set up the values in Properties, as shown in Figure 1–3.

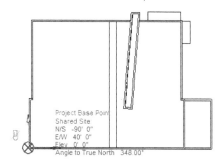

Figure 1–2

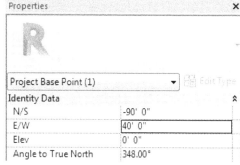

Figure 1–3

- The Project Base Point impacts absolute elevations, as well as what is reported using the **Spot Elevation** and **Spot Coordinate** commands.

- The Autodesk Revit software has a high level of accuracy of up to 20 miles from the project origin.

- If the Project Base Point is clipped ( ), the model element's project coordinates do not change when you move it. If it is unclipped ( ), the model element's project coordinates change.

New in 2017

- If you are linking in an Autodesk Revit project file, you can use the Positioning option **Auto Project Base Point to Project Base Point**.

1.2 Creating Topographical Surfaces

Once you have the Survey Point and Project Base Point in place, you can create topographical surfaces (toposurfaces), as shown in Figure 1–4.

- You can create a toposurface in three different ways:
    - Specify points directly in the project.
    - Import a CAD file with 3D information.
    - Import a points file (.txt or .cvs) developed by a surveyor.

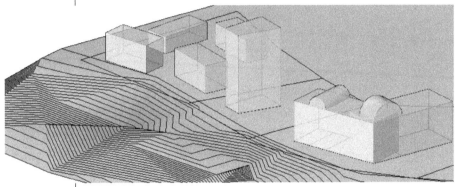

Figure 1–4

- You can edit toposurfaces by modifying individual points.

- Site settings that impact the toposurfaces include the contour line display and section graphics.

How To: Create a Toposurface By Specifying Points

1. Open a site or 3D view.
2. In the *Massing & Site* tab>Model Site panel, click  (Toposurface).
3. In the *Modify | Edit Surface* tab>Tools panel, click ⌂ (Place Point).
4. In the Options Bar, set the *Elevation* for the point as shown in Figure 1–5. By default, you are only able to select **Absolute Elevation**. After you create a surface of three points, you can also select **Relative to Surface**.

Figure 1–5

5. Click in the drawing area to place the point.
6. Continue placing points. You can vary the elevation as needed. After you have placed three points, a boundary is displayed, connecting them. When you add a point at a different elevation, you see the contour lines forming, as shown in Figure 1–6.

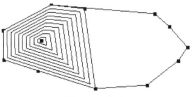

Figure 1–6

7. In the Surface panel, click (Finish Surface) when you have finished selecting points.

- Points can be added in plan and 3D views.

- To create a neat outer boundary for a toposurface, draw reference planes and then select points at the intersections of the planes.

How To: Create a Toposurface Using an Imported File

*When importing, do not use the **Current view only** option as you need the 3D information stored in the CAD file.*

1. In a site or 3D view, import a CAD file (DWG, DXF, or DGN) that holds the site information.
2. In the *Massing & Site* tab>Model Site panel, click

   (Toposurface).
3. In the *Modify | Edit Surface* tab>Tools panel, expand

   (Create from Import) and click (Select Import Instance).
4. Select the imported file by clicking on the edge of the file.
5. In the Add Points from Selected Layers dialog box, select the layers that hold the points (the layer names vary according to the original drawing file standard), as shown in Figure 1–7.

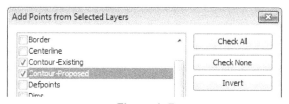

Figure 1–7

6. Click **OK**. The new toposurface is created with points at the same elevations as the imported information.

7. Click ✓ (Finish Surface) to end the command.

8. If you do not need the CAD file for other information, delete it.

- If the CAD file is going to be updated with information (such as the footprint of the building or roads and parking areas), it would be better to link the CAD file. This way, when the up-to-date information is provided, it is included in the project.

How To: Create a Toposurface from a Points File

1. Open a site or 3D view.

2. In the *Massing & Site* tab>Model Site panel, click

   ▨ (Toposurface).

3. In the *Modify | Edit Surface* tab>Tools panel, expand

   ▥ (Create from Import) and click ▤ (Specify Points File).

4. In the Select File dialog box, select the CSV or comma delimited text file (TXT) that contains the list of points and click **Open**.

5. In the Format dialog box, as shown in Figure 1–8, select the unit format and click **OK**. The options include **Decimal feet**, **Decimal inches**, **Meters**, **Centimeters**, and **Millimeters**.

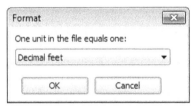

Figure 1–8

6. The points create a toposurface in the project. Add additional

   points as needed and click ✓ (Finish Surface).

- Having many points on a surface slows down system performance. While still in the *Modify | Edit Surface* tab>

   Tools panel, click ⬠ (Simplify Surface) to reduce the number of points. Set the required accuracy, as shown in Figure 1–9, and click **OK**.

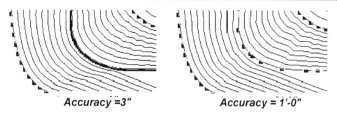

Accuracy = 3"   Accuracy = 1'-0"

Figure 1–9

Editing Toposurfaces

You can make changes to a toposurface by adding points or editing existing point locations and elevations, as shown in Figure 1–10. You can also modify the Properties of a toposurface, including material and phasing information.

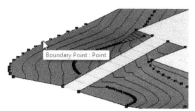

Figure 1–10

How To: Edit a Toposurface

1. Select the toposurface that you want to edit.

2. In the *Modify | Topography* tab>Surface panel, click (Edit Surface).

3. In the *Modify | Edit Surface* tab>Tools panel, click (Place Point) and add more points to the surface.

4. To edit existing points, select one or more points.

5. In the *Interior (or Boundary) Points* tab, you can use various modification tools. You can change the elevation of the points in the Options Bar, as shown in Figure 1–11.

When adding points, it helps to be in a 3D shaded view so that you can see the effects of your new points.

Figure 1–11

6. Select another point or click in an empty space to finish editing the points.

7. In the *Modify | Edit Surface* tab> Surface panel, click

 (Finish Surface) to end the command.

Site Settings

In the *Massing & Site* tab>Model Site panel, click ⌄ in the panel title. The Site Settings dialog box opens, in which you can set the way contours are displayed in the plan and section views of a toposurface, as shown in Figure 1–12.

Figure 1–12

Site Setting Options

Contour Line Display

At Intervals of:	Set the distance for the primary contour lines. These display with a heavy line and are not necessarily the places at which you added the points.
Passing Through Elevation	The starting elevation for contour lines.

Additional Contours

Start/Stop	**Start** is the location for a single additional contour or the first of a series of contours. **Stop** is the end of a series of additional contour lines.
Increment	The distance between sub-contours when the *Range type* is set to **Multiple Values**. The style is set according to the Subcategory specification.

Range Type	Set to **Multiple Values** or **Single Value**. When set to multiple, you can specify the start and stop and the increment. When set to **Single Value**, you can specify the location of the single contour in the **Start Value**. Increments are grayed out.
Subcategory	Select from a list of object styles that define how to display the additional contours. For example, **Secondary Contours** display with a thin line and **Primary Contours** with a wide line. You can create additional options in **Object Styles** under **Topography**.
Insert / Delete	Insert or delete additional contour descriptions.

Section Graphics

Section cut material	The default material is set to **Earth**. Click ▢ (Browse) to open the Material Browser in which you can select a different material. Additional site related materials can be found in the *AEC Materials: Misc* area at the bottom of the Material Browser. The following shows a section cut using the **Earth** material.
Elevation of poche base	The height of the poche (or hatching) that displays below the bottom contour line in a section view. It is usually negative.

Property Data

Angle Display	Select the type of angles to display: **Degrees from N/S** or **Degrees**.
Units	Select the type of units to display: **Degrees Minutes Seconds** or **Decimal Degrees**.

Practice 1a

Create Topographical Surfaces

Practice Objectives

- Import a CAD file with contours.
- Set the Project Base Point and the Survey Point.
- Create a Toposurface from the imported file.
- (Optional) Create a Toposurface using a Points file.

Estimated time for completion: 10 minutes

In this practice you will import a CAD file that contains contour information, set the Project Base Point and Survey Point, create a toposurface from the imported file, change the site settings, and add a section as shown in Figure 1–13.

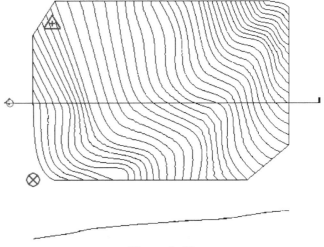

Figure 1–13

Task 1 - Import a CAD file.

1. Start a new project based on the default architectural template.

2. Open the **Floor Plans:Site** view.

3. In the *Insert* tab>Import panel, click (Import CAD).

This file was creating using the AutoCAD® software.

4. In the Import CAD Formats dialog box, navigate to the practice files folder and select **Site-DWG.dwg**. Accept the default options and click **Open**.

5. Type **ZE** to zoom out to the extents of the file. The origin of the imported CAD file is placed at the origin of the project, as shown in Figure 1–14.

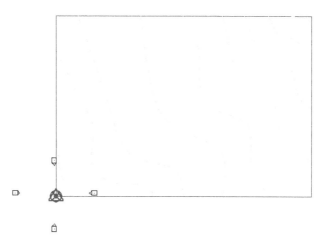

Figure 1–14

6. Save the project in the practice files folder as **New-Site.rvt**.

Task 2 - Set the Project Base Point and the Survey Point.

1. Click on the Project Base Point and set the information as shown in Figure 1–15, and as follows:
   - N/S: **63' 0"**
   - E/W: **75' 0"**
   - Elev: **1856' 0"**
   - Angle to True North: **20 degrees**

This is information you would receive from surveyors or civil engineers.

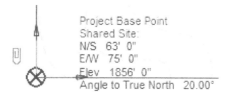

Figure 1–15

2. The project elements move with the Project Base Point. Type **ZE** again to display the new location of the site.

3. Select the Survey Point and click 🔖 to unclip it.

4. Set the information as shown in Figure 1–16, and as follows:
   - N/S: **354' 0"**
   - E/W: **225' 0"**
   - Elev: **1864' 0"**

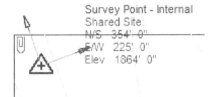

Figure 1–16

5. Reclip the Survey Point in its new location.

6. Hide the elevation markers and save the project

Task 3 - Create a Toposurface from the Imported file.

---

1. Continue working in the **Floor Plans: Site** view.

2. In the *Massing & Site* tab>Model Site panel, click (Toposurface).

3. In the *Modify | Edit Surface* tab>Tools panel, expand (Create from Import) and click (Select Import Instance).

4. Select the imported CAD file.

5. In the Add Points from Selected Layers dialog box, click **Check None**. Select the layer **Contour-Existing** (as shown in Figure 1–17) and click **OK**.

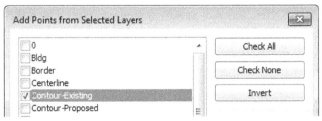

Figure 1–17

6. The new toposurface is created with points applied along the contour lines from the CAD file, as shown in Figure 1–18.

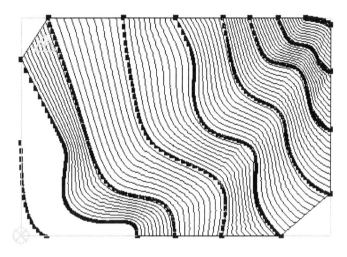

Figure 1–18

7. In the *Modify | Edit Surface* tab> Tools panel click (Simplify Surface).

8. In the Simplify Surface dialog box, set the *Accuracy* to **1'-0"** (as shown in Figure 1–19) and click **OK**.

Figure 1–19

9. Fewer points are placed in the toposurface without compromising the actual contour location. Click (Finish Surface).

10. Hide the linked CAD file.

11. The contour lines are closer together than the ones displayed in the CAD file, as shown in Figure 1–20. This distance is specified in the Site Settings.

12. In the *Massing & Site* tab>Model Site panel title, click ⌐ (Site Settings).

13. In the Site Settings dialog box, in the *Additional Contours* area, set the *Increment* to **2'-0"**, and click **OK**. The distance between the contours changes, as shown in Figure 1–21.

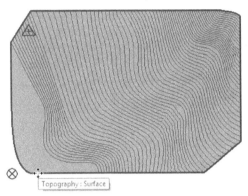

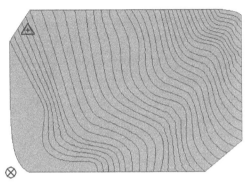

Figure 1–20   Figure 1–21

14. Save the project.

Task 4 - Create a Site Section.

1. In the *View* tab>Create panel, click ⌐ (Section) and draw a horizontal section through the site.

2. In the Project Browser, in the *Section (Building Section)* node, rename the section as **Site Section**.

3. Open the section view. The material displayed in the section is **Earth**, as shown in Figure 1–22, which was specified in the Site Settings.

Figure 1–22

4. Save the project.

Task 5 - (Optional) Create a Toposurface using a Points file.

1. Using Notepad or another text editor, in the practice files folder, open **Topography-Points.txt**. The list of points, shown in part in Figure 1–23, includes three numbers on each line. The format is **Northing (Y), Easting (X), Elevation (ft)**.

```
Topography-Points.txt - Notepad
File  Edit  Format  View  Help
4999.9900,4999.9900,620.0775
4717.8383,5016.3942,636.4817
4658.7833,4589.8858,590.5500
4343.8233,4655.5025,623.3583
4255.2408,4557.0775,629.9200
4288.0492,4265.0833,616.7967
4288.0492,4045.2675,613.5158
4288.0492,3799.2050,590.5500
4124.0075,3832.0133,606.9542
3920.5958,3845.1367,616.7967
3763.1158,3841.8558,620.0775
3625.3208,3861.5408,646.3242
```

Figure 1–23

2. Close the text file.

3. In the practice files folder, open **Topography-Points.rvt**.

4. Open the **Elevations (Building Elevation): South** view.

5. There are two levels. *Level 1* is set to **700'**, which works best with the information provided in the points file for the elevation, which ranges from 590 to 744 feet.

6. Open the default 3D view.

7. In the *Massing & Site* tab>Model Site panel, click

   (Toposurface).

8. In the *Modify | Edit Surface* tab>Tools panel, expand

   (Create from Import) and click (Specify Points File).

9. In the Open dialog box, set the *Files of type* to **Comma delimited Text** and select **Topography-Points.txt.** Click **Open**.

10. In the Format dialog box, select **Decimal feet** and click **OK**.

11. Type **ZE** to zoom to the extents of the file.

12. Click ✓ (Finish Surface).

13. Zoom in on the toposurface and investigate it.

14. Modify the Site Settings, Material, and Visual Style as needed to get a better understanding of the site as shown in Figure 1–24.

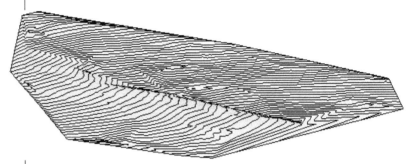

Figure 1–24

15. Save and close the project.

1.3 Adding Property Lines and Building Pads

When you have placed the base toposurface, you need to add the property lines and building pad (the cutout for the building location), as shown in Figure 1–25.

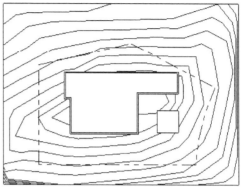

Figure 1–25

Creating Property Lines

Property lines can be created by sketching lines or inputting information into a table of distances and bearings.

*   Property lines can, but do not need to be, drawn on a toposurface.

How To: Add a Property Line

1. In the *Massing & Site* tab>Modify Site panel, click
    (Property Line).
2. In the Create Property Line dialog box, select how you want to create the property line, as shown in Figure 1–26.

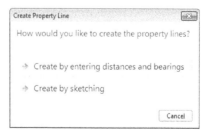

Figure 1–26

3. If you selected **Create by sketching**, use the Draw tools to create the property line, and click 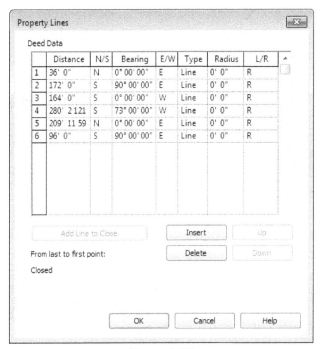 (Finish Edit Mode). If you selected **Create by entering distances and bearings**, fill out the appropriate information, as shown in Figure 1–27, and click **OK** to finish.

Property Lines

Deed Data

	Distance	N/S	Bearing	E/W	Type	Radius	L/R
1	36' 0"	N	0° 00' 00"	E	Line	0' 0"	R
2	172' 0"	S	90° 00' 00"	E	Line	0' 0"	R
3	164' 0"	S	0° 00' 00"	W	Line	0' 0"	R
4	280' 2 121	S	73° 00' 00"	W	Line	0' 0"	R
5	209' 11 59	N	0° 00' 00"	E	Line	0' 0"	R
6	96' 0"	S	90° 00' 00"	E	Line	0' 0"	R

Add Line to Close   Insert   Up

From last to first point: Delete   Down

Closed

OK   Cancel   Help

Figure 1–27

- When typing the bearings, you do not need to insert the symbols after the numbers, just separate them with a space. For example, 54 23 47 displays as 54° 23' 47".

- Property lines do not need to close to be inserted into the drawing. Not all of the information you receive for a deed or survey adds up to a closed property line. Click **Add Line to Close**, as required.

- A sketched property line can be converted into a table. Select the property line, and in the *Modify | Property Lines* tab> Property Lines panel, click (Edit Table). When it has been converted it cannot go back to a sketch.

Creating Building Pads

A building pad on a toposurface cuts or fills the surface around the area of the pad. You can create the pad from existing walls or sketch it with lines. The example in Figure 1–28 shows the site with a building pad in section.

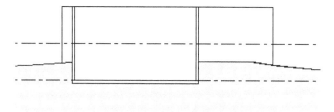

Figure 1–28

- A pad is an element in the project that might be in the same plane as a floor.

- A pad affects the surrounding surface and a floor element does not.

- Pads can be turned off in the Visibility/Graphic Overrides dialog box.

How To: Create a Building Pad

1. Open the site plan view with an existing toposurface. Building pads must be drawn on a toposurface.
2. In the *Massing & Site* tab>Model Site panel, click

   (Building Pad).
3. In the *Modify | Create Pad Boundary* tab>Draw panel, click

   (Boundary Line). You can use any of the Draw tools or click (Pick Walls) to establish the outline of the building pad.
4. In Properties, specify a *Level* and a *Height Offset from Level* for the depth of the pad and set any phasing as needed.

5. Click (Finish Edit Mode).

- The sketch of a pad must form a closed loop, but can contain additional loops inside to display openings (such as a courtyard). If you have several buildings, create a pad for each one.

- You can slope pads in one direction for drainage using

   (Slope Arrow).

Practice 1b

Add Property Lines and Building Pads

Practice Objectives

- Create a property line by sketching.
- Add a building pad.

Estimated time for completion: 10 minutes

In this practice you will add a property line and a building pad to a toposurface, as shown in Figure 1–29.

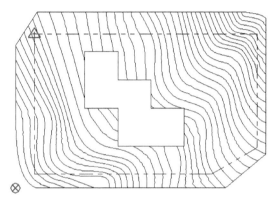

Figure 1–29

Task 1 - Create a property lines.

1. In the practice files folder, open **New-Site-Pad.rvt**.

2. Open the **Site** plan view if it is not already open.

3. In the *Massing & Site* tab>Modify Site panel, click

   (Property Line).

4. In the Create Property Line dialog box, select **Create by sketching** as shown in Figure 1–30.

Figure 1–30

5. Sketch the property line, as shown in Figure 1–31.

Use the Survey Point as the start point of the property line.

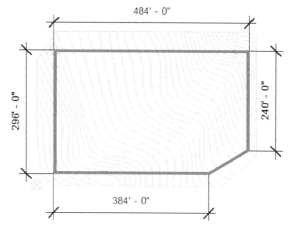

Figure 1–31

6. Click ✓ (Finish Edit Mode).

Task 2 - Create a building pad.

---

1. In the *Massing & Site* tab>Model Site panel, click
   ▣ (Building Pad).

2. In the *Modify | Create Pad Boundary* tab>Draw panel, click
   ⌐ (Boundary Line). Use the Draw tools to establish the
   outline of the building pad, as shown in Figure 1–32.

Use the Survey Point to identify the start point of the pad.

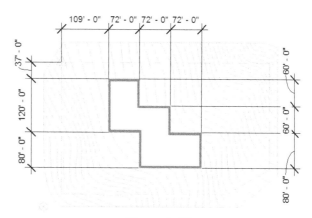

Figure 1–32

3. In Properties, verify that the *Level* is **Level 1** and the *Height Offset from Level* is set to **0**.

4. Click  (Finish Edit Mode).

5. Open the **Site Section** view and see how the pad cuts the site, as shown in Figure 1–33.

Figure 1–33

6. Save the project.

1.4 Modifying Toposurfaces

Building a new structure requires that the earth around it be moved to make space for the building and to promote drainage. This means you need to modify the toposurface beyond just introducing the building pad, and applying different materials, as shown in Figure 1–34. You can use commands to finalize the site design, such as **Subregion**, **Split Surface**, and **Graded Region**.

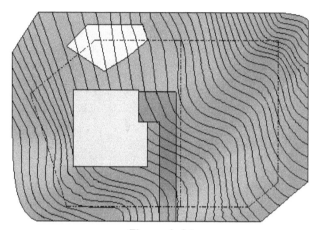

Figure 1–34

Creating Subregions

When you submit a preliminary proposal, you might want to display different materials on parts of the toposurface without changing the contours. You can quickly create subregions of the surface and apply different materials to them, as shown in Figure 1–34.

How To: Create a Subregion

1. In the *Massing & Site* tab>Modify Site panel, click

   (Subregion).
2. In the *Modify | Create Subregion Boundary* tab>Draw panel, use the Draw tools to outline the subregion.
3. In Properties, modify the *Material* for the subregion as needed.

4. Click   (Finish Edit Mode).
5. The subregion is still selected, In Properties specify a material, if you did not do it before.

*The subregions display with a boundary, but are still part of the main toposurface. Set the Visual Style to **Shaded**, **Consistent Colors**, or **Realistic** to display the colors of the materials.*

- To modify a subregion, in the *Modify Topography* tab>Subregion panel, click (Edit Boundary).

- To remove a subregion, select it but do not edit the boundary. Press <Delete>.

Splitting Surfaces

 (Split Surface) is a more powerful command that breaks toposurfaces into separate pieces. Each surface can be edited individually and be assigned different materials, as shown in Figure 1–35.

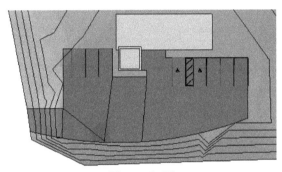

Figure 1–35

For example, you can break the topography into sections for parking lots, grassy areas, roadways, and sidewalks. You can also delete sections that you do not need in the project.

How To: Split a Surface

1. In the *Massing & Site* tab>Modify Site panel, click (Split Surface).
2. Select the toposurface to split.
3. In the *Modify | Split Surface* tab>Draw panel, use the Draw tools to create a splitting boundary.
4. In Properties, modify the *Material* for the surface as needed.

5. Click (Finish Edit Mode).

- The boundary does not need to be a closed object, but must split the surface into two pieces.

How To: Join Surfaces

1. In the *Massing & Site* tab>Modify Site panel, click  (Merge Surfaces).
2. Select the two adjacent surfaces that you want to merge.

- If materials are applied to the surfaces, the new merged surface takes on the material of the first selected surface.

Grading a Site

The most time-consuming part of site work is deciding how to grade a site and adjusting the contours accordingly. You can make sections of the site flatter or steeper and you always need to verify that the drainage pattern flows away from the building and towards the storm drains. To make this process easier, use

the (Graded Region) command to modify the location of points and then automatically demolish and add contours.

- Graded regions change the phase of the toposurface. In Properties, set the *Phase* of the original toposurface to **Existing** (as shown in Figure 1–36) before starting the **Graded Region** command.

Phasing	⌃
Phase Created	Existing
Phase Demolished	None

Figure 1–36

- When you modify topography with the **Graded Region** command, the software automatically calculates the Cut and Fill for the surface. This information is displayed in Properties (as shown in Figure 1–37) and can be added to a schedule.

Phasing		⌃
Phase Created	New Construction	
Phase Demolished	None	
Other		⌃
Net cut/fill	-14782.56 CF	
Fill	8143.94 CF	
Cut	22926.49 CF	

Figure 1–37

How To: Grade a Site

1. Verify that the *Phase* of the toposurface is set to **Existing**.
2. In the *Massing & Site* tab>Modify Site panel, click

   ⬆ (Graded Region).
3. The Edit Graded Region dialog box opens, as shown in Figure 1–38. Select how you want the new toposurface to be copied. You have the option of creating a replica of the original or an outline of the points.

The existing toposurface is automatically demolished and a new copy is created in its place.

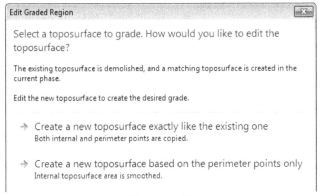

Figure 1–38

4. Select the toposurface that you want to grade.
5. Modify the points in the surface:
   - In the *Modify | Edit Surface* tab Tools panel click

     🏠 (Place Point) to add new points.
   - Select a point and in the Options Bar change the *Elevation*.
   - Delete points that are no longer needed.

6. Click ✔ (Finish Surface).

- If the surface is open or there is a conflict, an alert box opens.

- If you are in a shaded view, the demolished area displays in red. Set the *Visual Style* to **Hidden** to display the contours and points more clearly.

1.5 Annotating Site Plans

Site plan annotation can include information about setbacks, dimensions, and spaces for the various site components, utility and grading information, etc. Most of this information can be added with standard tools, such as **Text** and **Dimensions**. There are several annotation items that work with site plans: **Label Contours** (shown in Figure 1–39), **Spot Elevation**, and **Spot Coordinate**.

Label Contours *only works with toposurfaces.*

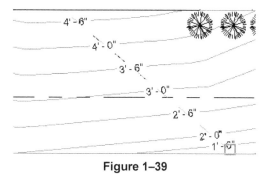

Figure 1–39

Labeling Contours

Labeling the contours can help the process of grading regions by displaying the level of the contour lines in the region in which you are working.

How To: Label Contours

1. In the *Massing & Site* tab>Modify Site panel, click ⟋⁵⁰ (Label Contours).
2. Draw a line across the contours that you want to label.
3. Continue drawing as many lines as needed.

Hint: Viewing a True North Site Plan

When you are ready to annotate and place a site plan on a sheet, you can create a view displaying the rotation to True North, as shown in Figure 1–40.

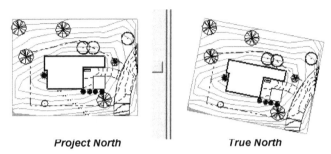

Project North   *True North*

Figure 1–40

1. Create a copy of the plan view that you want to rotate to true north. You can tile the views so that they both display.
2. In the Properties of the true north plan, set the *Orientation* to **True North**, as shown in Figure 1–41.

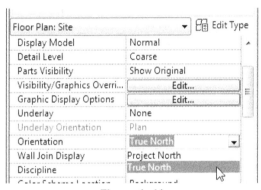

Figure 1–41

3. The view rotates to match the **True North** specified in the Project Base Point.

Add Spot Dimensions

All dimensions are based on the Project Base Point.

These dimensioning tools display important information about specific points on your toposurface, as shown in Figure 1–42. **Spot Elevation** gathers the elevation information from a selected point while **Spot Coordinate** gathers the coordinate information for a point.

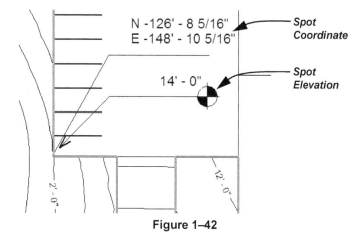

Figure 1–42

- Spot dimensions can be added on any type of model element, not just toposurfaces.

How To: Add Spot Elevations/Coordinates

1. In the *Annotate* tab>Dimension panel, click ⤹ (Spot Elevation) or ⊕ (Spot Coordinate).
2. In the Type Selector, select the type that you want to use from the list, as shown in Figure 1–43.

Figure 1–43

3. In the Options Bar, select the **Leader** and **Shoulder** options. The Spot Coordinate also includes a list of **Display Elevations** as shown in Figure 1–44.

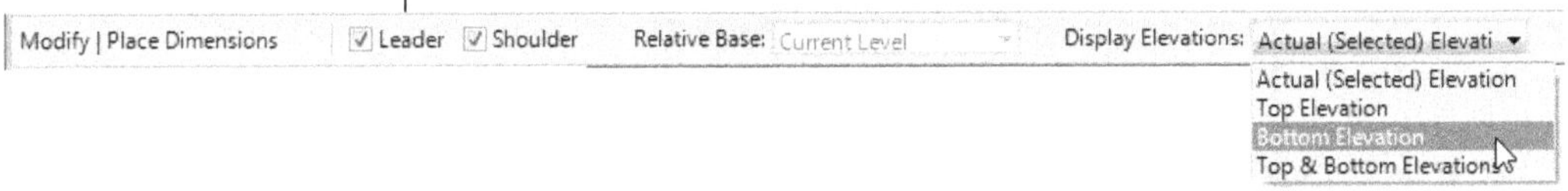

Figure 1–44

4. Select a point to dimension and place the leader line and target or text. The software automatically gathers the information from the selected point.
5. Select another point as needed. The value of the spot dimension displays as you move the cursor over the site.

Practice 1c | Modify Toposurfaces

Practice Objectives

- Split surfaces and change the material of an existing toposurface.
- Grade surfaces to create an even patio with a sunken pool.
- Grade the slope of the parking lot and driveway.

Estimated time for completion: 20 minutes

In this practice you will use **Split Surface** to add several new surfaces, **Label Contours** to prepare contours for modification, and **Graded Region** to modify the points within a graded region, as shown in Figure 1–45.

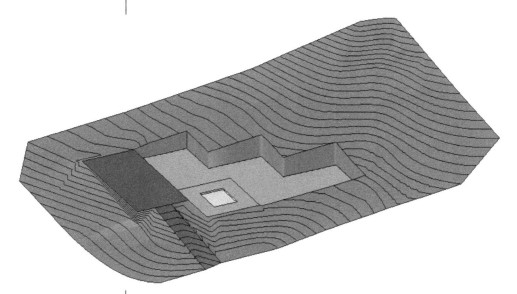

Figure 1–45

Task 1 - Split Surfaces and Change the Material.

1. In the practice files folder, open **New-Site-Modify.rvt**.

2. Ensure that you are in the **Floor Plans: Site** view.

3. In the View Control Bar, set the *Visual Style* to (Shaded).

4. In the *Massing & Site* tab>Modify Site panel, click (Split Surface).

5. Select the toposurface.

6. Draw the boundary for the patio as shown in Figure 1–46.

Figure 1–46

7. In the *Modify | Split Surface* tab> Mode panel, click

   ✓ (Finish Edit Mode).

8. Start the **Split Surface** command and create the surfaces for the reflecting pool and parking area, as shown in Figure 1–47.

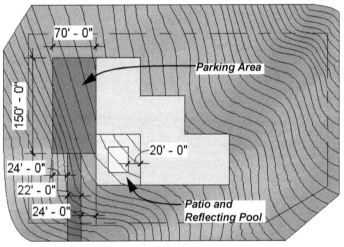

Figure 1–47

9. Using Properties, assign the following materials to each surface:

   • Patio: **Masonry – Stone**

   • Parking Area: **Site-Asphalt**

   • Reflecting Pool: **Site – Water**

   • Main Site: **Site – Grass**

10. Save the project.

Task 2 - Grade Surfaces.

1. Select all of the topography surfaces. In Properties, set *Phase Created* to **Existing**. This is important for grading the surfaces. If you have the view shaded, they all turn gray.

2. Zoom in on the patio.

3. In the *Massing & Site* tab>Modify Site panel, click

    ⟟ (Graded Region).

4. In the Edit Graded Region dialog box, select **Create a new toposurface exactly like the existing one**.

5. Select the patio surface.

To select more than one point at a time, draw a window around them.

6. Delete all the points except those on the corners of the patio and the corners of the pool. This flattens the patio surface.

7. Select all of the corner points. In the Options Bar, set the *Elevation* to **14'-0"**.

8. In the *Modify | Edit Surface* tab> Surface panel, click

    ✎ (Finish Surface). If you have the view shaded, the cut areas display in red, as shown in Figure 1–48.

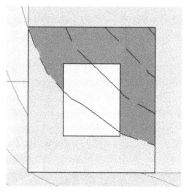

Figure 1–48

9. Start the Graded Region command and select the pool.

10. In the Edit Graded Region dialog box, select **Create a new toposurface exactly like the existing one**.

11. Delete the extra points and set the *Elevation* of the corner points of the pool to **12'-0"**.

12. Save the project.

Task 3 - Modify the Slope of the Parking Lot and Driveway .

1. In Properties, in the *Phasing* area, change the *Phase Filter* to **Show Complete**. This helps you to see what you are doing.

2. In the *Massing & Site* tab>Modify Site panel, click ^{.50} (Label Contours). Label the contours on either side of the driveway, as shown in Figure 1–49. (Change the view scale as needed to display the labels without them being in the way.)

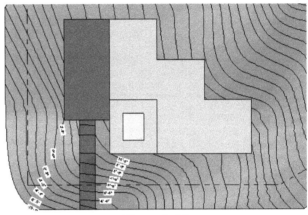

Figure 1–49

3. In the *Massing & Site* tab>Modify Site panel, click

    (Graded Region) and select **Create a new toposurface based on the perimeter points only**.

4. Select the parking area and use the procedure that you used with the patio: delete all of the points except the corner points, and set those points to **14'-0"**.

5. The driveway is sloped from **14'-0**" at the top to (negative) **-4-0"** at the bottom. Delete any excess points and modify the rest.

6. Click   (Finish Surface) when you are finished.

7. As time permits, repeat the process with the grassy area so that it butts up against the flat and sloped surfaces as needed. Modify points to change the slope away from the driveway.

8. Save the project.

1.6 Adding Site Components

When you have established a site with surfaces and building pads, you need to populate it with other site elements, such as parking spaces and trees. Site components are inserted as with any other component. However, instead of taking on the current level when they are inserted, they link to the elevation of the contour where they are placed, as shown in Figure 1–50.

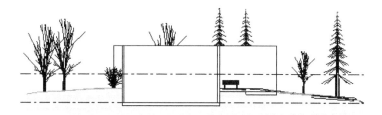

Figure 1–50

- To access site components, click ⌂ (Site Component) or
  ▦ (Parking Component) in the *Massing & Site* tab>Model Site panel.

- To load different types of components, in the *Insert* tab>Load from Library panel, use ⬇ (Load Family).

- The Autodesk Revit family library includes the *Site* folder with sub-folders for *Accessories*, *Logistics*, *Parking*, and *Utilities*.
  - *Accessories* include items such as bike stands and trash cans.
  - *Logistics* includes trucks, cranes, and other construction equipment.
  - *Parking* includes parking spaces, islands, direction arrows, and an ADA-compliant curb cut, parking space, and symbol.
  - *Utilities* includes catch basins, fire hydrants, manhole covers, and more.

- Additional trees and shrubs can be loaded from the Library in the *Planting* folder. Each family (Shrub, Conifer, and Deciduous) contains a variety of types and heights of trees.

- Many components, not just site specific components, are face-based and can use a toposurface as a host if they are added in a view in which the toposurface is visible.

- If the site component is not visible after you finish attaching it to the site, click (Pick New Host) in the associated *Modify* tab>Host panel, and verify that the component is associated with the correct surface. If **Pick Host** does not work, change the elevation of the component in Properties.

Practice 1d

Add Site Components

Practice Objective

Estimated time for completion: 10 minutes

- Add trees, parking spaces, and the ADA symbol to a toposurface.

In this practice you will add parking spaces, ADA symbols, and trees, as shown in Figure 1–51.

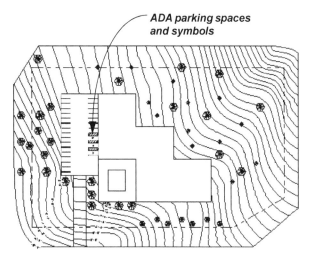

ADA parking spaces and symbols

Figure 1–51

Task 1 - Add Site components.

1. In the practice files folder, open **New-Site-Components.rvt**.

2. In the *Insert* tab>Load from Library panel, click (Load Family).

3. In the Load Family dialog box, in the Autodesk Revit Library, navigate to the *Site>Parking* folder and select **Parking Space - ADA.rfa** and **Parking Symbol - ADA.rfa**. Click **Open**.

4. In the *Massing & Site* tab>Model Site panel, click

   (Parking Component) and place the ADA parking spaces and other parking spaces, as shown in Figure 1–51.

5. In the *Massing & Site* tab>Model Site panel, click (Site Component) and place the ADA symbol within the parking spaces.

6. Continue using the **Site Component** command and add trees around the property using various types and heights.

7. Add other components as required. These can include site accessories such as bollards and planters, or parking symbols such as direction arrows,

Task 2 - View the Completed Model

1. Open a 3D view and set the *Visual Style* to **Shaded**.

2. In Properties, set the *Phase Filter* to **Show Complete**.

3. Rotate the 3D view.

4. You can also add retaining walls or other building features.

5. Save the project.

1.7 Working with Shared Positioning

Each project created in the Autodesk Revit Architecture software has a set of internal coordinates that are only used by that project. As long as you are working in a stand-alone project, you do not need to reference these coordinates. However, if you are linking projects together, you might want to have one coordinate system that is referenced throughout the connected projects. This is when you need to share coordinates.

The Project Base Point, typically visible in a site plan, establishes the coordinate system.

- Shared Sites can be specified in the Properties of the linked model, as shown in Figure 1–52.

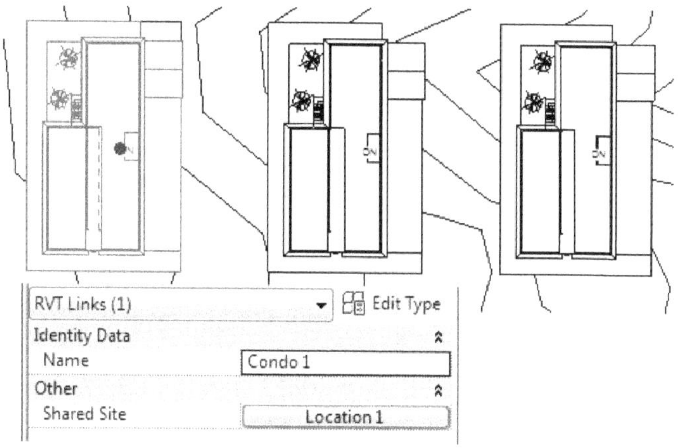

Figure 1–52

- Linked models that share coordinates can be created in the Autodesk Revit software or a combination of files created in the Autodesk Revit software and DWG and DXF files created in the AutoCAD software.

- Shared coordinates should only be derived from one file. You can acquire coordinates from a linked project or drawing or publish them from the host project to the other files.

Publishing and Acquiring Coordinates

Shared coordinates are most often used with site plans to which multiple buildings are linked. The buildings can all be different or can be copies of the same project, such as in an apartment complex. The site project typically controls the coordinates.

- If you are working in the site project, you can select the links and publish the coordinates to them.

- If you are working in a building project, you can acquire the coordinates from the site project.

Enhanced
in **2017**

- Typically, the architectural project acquires the coordinates from a site project and the other disciplines then link the architectural model into their projects using **Origin to Origin** or **Project Base Point to Project Base Point**.

How To: Publish Coordinates to Linked Models

1. Open the host project whose coordinates you want to use, which contains the linked models.
2. In the *Manage* tab>Project Location panel, expand

   ⌐ (Coordinates) and click ↱ (Publish Coordinates).
3. Select the linked model to which you want to publish the shared coordinate system. The Location Weather and Site dialog box opens with the *Site* tab active, as shown in Figure 1–53.

Click ⊕ (Location) in the Manage tab>Project Location panel to open the dialog box at any time.

Figure 1–53

4. The Internal named location of the linked model is the default. Click **Rename...** to give the default location a different name. Click **Duplicate...** to create a new name for the instance location. Each instance of the linked model should have a differently named location.
5. Select the location that you want to use and click **OK**.
6. You are still in the command and can select another linked project to which to publish the coordinates or press <Esc> to end the command.

- You only need to publish coordinates to a linked model once. However, you can use this method on multiple instances to create the named locations.

How To: Save the Modifications to the Linked Model

When the coordinates have been published, they still need to be saved to the linked model.

1. In the *Manage* tab>Manage Project panel, click 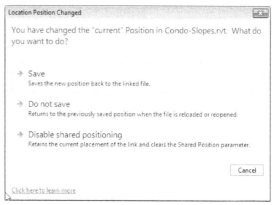 (Manage Links).
2. In the Manage Links dialog box, select the *Revit* tab.
3. A check mark displays in the *Positions Not Saved* column, as shown in Figure 1–54, indicating that the published coordinates have not yet been saved to the linked model.

Linked File	Status	Reference Type	Positions Not Saved
Townhouse.r	Loaded	Overlay	☑

Figure 1–54

4. Select the name in the *Linked File* column and click **Save Positions**.
5. In the Location Position Changed dialog box shown in Figure 1–55, select the method that you want to use.

Location Position Changed

You have changed the "current" Position in Condo-Slopes.rvt. What do you want to do?

→ Save
Saves the new position back to the linked file.

→ Do not save
Returns to the previously saved position when the file is reloaded or reopened.

→ Disable shared positioning
Retains the current placement of the link and clears the Shared Position parameter.

Cancel

Click here to learn more

Figure 1–55

6. If you selected **Save**, the **Positions Not Saved** option is cleared in the Manage Links dialog box
7. Click **OK** to close the dialog box.

- If you make a change to the location or save the project before managing the links, you are prompted to make a selection in the same dialog box.

Acquiring Coordinates

If you are working in a project with linked models and want to use the coordinates from one of the linked models rather than from the host project, you can acquire the coordinates, as shown in Figure 1–56. For example, you might have a drawing site plan that was created in the AutoCAD software linked to a project created in the Autodesk Revit Architecture software and want to use the coordinates from the DWG file.

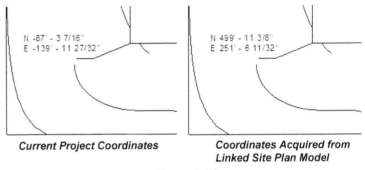

Current Project Coordinates   **Coordinates Acquired from Linked Site Plan Model**

Figure 1–56

How To: Acquire Coordinates from a Linked Project

1. In the *Manage* tab>Project Location panel, expand

   (Coordinates) and click (Acquire Coordinates).
2. Select a linked model from which to acquire the shared coordinate system. The current project now uses the new coordinates.

- If you move or rotate a linked instance after it has been shared and saved, a Warning box opens as shown in Figure 1–57. You can click **Save Now** to save the position or click **OK** to continue working in the project. You can save the linked model later using the Manage Links dialog box.

Figure 1–57

Selecting Locations

It is possible to select locations for multiple instances of linked models using the **Publish Coordinates** command. Another way of specifying locations is to use the Properties of the linked model. If you have not already published coordinates to the linked project, you are prompted to reconcile the link before proceeding. Through Properties, you can move a linked instance to a new location, record the current position to a named location, or stop sharing the location of the linked instance.

How To: Select or Specify a Named Location for a linked model

1. Select the linked model.
2. In Properties, next to *Shared Site*, click **<Not Shared>**.
3. If the linked model is already reconciled, the Select Location dialog box opens, as shown in Figure 1–58.

Figure 1–58

- You can move the instance to an existing named location. Select **Move instance to:** and select the location from the list.
- If you do not want to select a named location, select **Do not share location of selected instance**.

- If you need to create a new named location, select **Record current position...** and click **Change....** The Location Weather and Site dialog box opens, in which you can create a new named location as shown in Figure 1–59. Make the new location current.

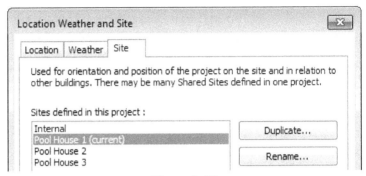

Figure 1–59

4. Click **OK** to close the dialog box.
5. The value of the **Shared Site** option is now the new location name, as shown in Figure 1–60.

Figure 1–60

Hint: Identifying Coordinates

To identify a coordinate point: in the *Manage* tab>Project Location panel, expand ⌐ (Coordinates) and click ⌐ (Report Shared Coordinates). ⌐ displays on the cursor. Move it over a point on the project and click on it. The Shared Coordinates display in the Options Bar, as shown in Figure 1–61.

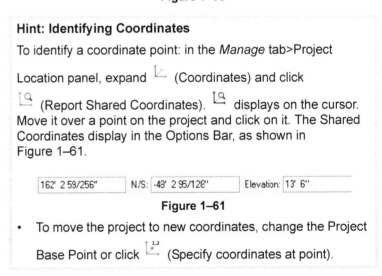

Figure 1–61

- To move the project to new coordinates, change the Project Base Point or click ⌐ (Specify coordinates at point).

Reconciling Links

When you select a linked model and in Properties, select **Shared Site**, and the link has not been reconciled with the host project, the Share Coordinates dialog box opens, as shown in Figure 1–62.

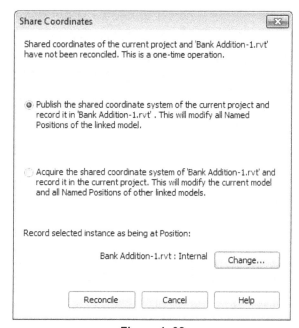

Figure 1–62

- This only occurs the first time you select a file that does not share coordinates. If you select other instances of the same link, this dialog box does not open.

How To: Reconcile Links

1. In the Share Coordinates dialog box, select **Publish** or **Acquire**.
2. Click **Change...** to record the location of the instance.
3. In the Location Weather and Site dialog box, specify the named location and click **OK**.
4. In the Share Coordinates dialog box, click **Reconcile**.

Practice 1e

Work With Shared Positioning

Practice Objectives

- Link a model to a site host project multiple times.
- Publish Coordinates and Share Locations.
- Test different locations

Estimated time for completion: 15 minutes

In this practice you will link a project to a site multiple times, publish coordinates, and share locations. You will also test different locations using shared coordinates, as shown in Figure 1–63.

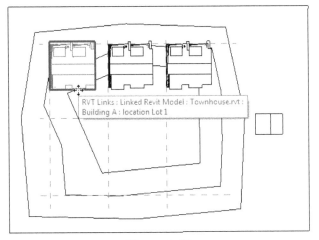

Figure 1–63

Task 1 - Link a Model to a Site multiple times.

1. In the practice files folder, open **Townhouse-Site.rvt**.

2. In the *Insert* tab>Link panel, click ![icon](Link Revit).

3. In the Import/Link RVT dialog box, select **Townhouse.rvt** with the *Positioning:* set to **Auto-Origin to Origin**.

4. Move the link so that the upper left corner meets the intersection of the two reference planes, as shown in Figure 1–64.

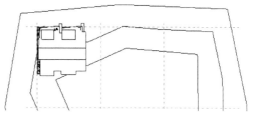

Figure 1–64

5. Copy the link to the other two reference plane intersections, as shown in Figure 1–65.

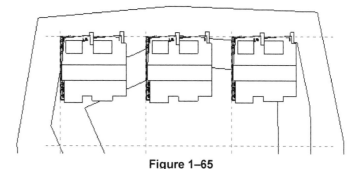

Figure 1–65

6. Select the first link. In Properties, set the value of the *Name* to **Building A**, as shown in Figure 1–66. Do not modify the **Shared Site** at this time.

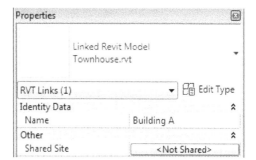

Figure 1–66

7. Repeat the process with the other two instances of the linked model. Name them **Building B** and **Building C**.

Task 2 - Publish Coordinates and Share Locations.

1. In the *Manage* tab>Project Location panel, expand ∟ (Coordinates) and click ⇨ (Publish Coordinates).

2. Select **Building A**.

3. In the Location Weather and Site dialog box, in the *Site* tab, click **Rename...**. Rename the location as **Lot 1**, as shown in Figure 1–67.

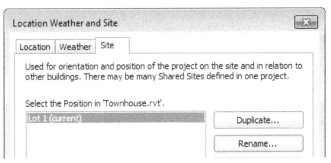

Figure 1–67

4. Click **OK** and click ⟶ (Modify) to end the command. (You could continue using the **Publish Coordinates** command to assign named locations to the other instances of the link, but the next steps show you how to do it using Properties.)

5. Select **Building B**. In Properties, next to *Shared Site*, click **<Not Shared>**

6. Select **Record current position...** and click **Change...**.

7. Click **Duplicate...** to create a new named location named **Lot 2**.

8. Click **OK** twice to close the dialog boxes. The *Shared Site* is now set to **Lot 2**.

9. Repeat the process with the third link.

10. In the *Manage* tab>Manage Project panel, click ⌗ (Manage Links).

11. In the Manage Links dialog box, select the *Revit* tab.

12. The **Positions Not Saved** option is selected in the list (as shown in Figure 1–68) indicating that the published coordinates have not been saved to the linked model.

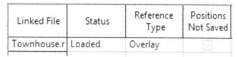

Linked File	Status	Reference Type	Positions Not Saved
Townhouse.r	Loaded	Overlay	☐

Figure 1–68

13. Select the *Linked File* name **Townhouse.rvt** and click **Save Positions**.

14. In the Location Position Changed dialog box shown in Figure 1–69, select **Save**.

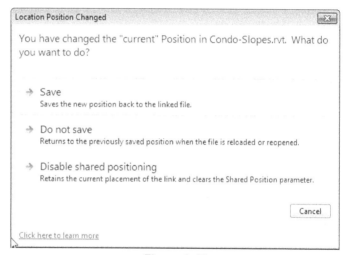

Figure 1–69

15. The **Positions Not Saved** option is cleared. Click **OK** to close the Manage Links dialog box.

16. Zoom out to display the entire site.

17. Do not close the project.

Task 3 - Test different locations.

1. In the practice files folder, open **Poolhouse.rvt**.

2. In the *Manage* tab>Project Location panel, click
   (Location).

---

3. In the Location Weather and Site dialog box, in the *Site* tab, three named locations are listed in addition to the **Internal** location, as shown in Figure 1–70. These were created when the model was previously linked to the host site project.

Figure 1–70

4. Close the dialog box, close the project, and verify that you are in the **Townhouse-Site.rvt** project.

5. In the *Insert* tab>Link panel, click (Link Revit).

6. Select the **Poolhouse.rvt** project. Set *Positioning:* to **Auto-By Shared Coordinates**, as shown in Figure 1–71, and click **Open**.

Figure 1–71

7. In the Location Weather and Site dialog box, in the *Site* tab, select one of the named locations and click **OK**. The pool house is automatically inserted at that location.

8. Select the pool house.

9. In Properties, click the button next to *Shared Site*.

10. In the Choose Site dialog box, select **Move Instance to:** and select one of the other named locations in the list, as shown in Figure 1–72.

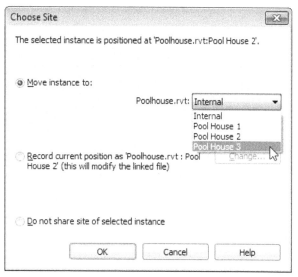

Figure 1–72

11. Close the dialog boxes. The pool house moves to the named location. The three locations are shown in Figure 1–73.

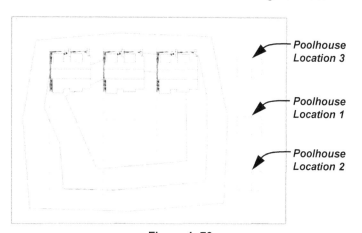

Figure 1–73

12. Save and close the project.

Chapter Review Questions

1. In which of the following ways can you NOT create topographical surfaces, such as that shown in Figure 1–74?

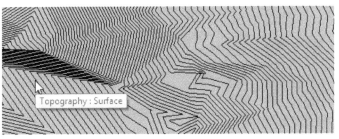

Figure 1–74

   a. From an imported drawing that was creating using the AutoCAD® software.

   b. By sketching.

   c. From an imported drawing that was created using the AutoCAD® Civil 3D® software.

   d. From a points file.

2. Which of the following commands enables you to modify a toposurface so that you can change various parts of the surface to different materials (as shown in Figure 1–75), and to modify the contours separately from the main toposurface?

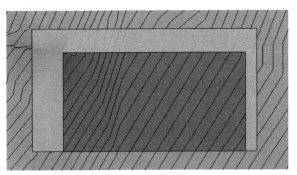

Figure 1–75

   a. Edit Surface

   b. Graded Region

   c. Merge Surface

   d. Split Surface

3. Which of the following defines the origin of the project coordinate system and impacts absolute elevations?

a. Project Origin

b. Survey Point

c. Project Base Point

d. Survey Base Point

4. Which of the following best describes the difference between a building pad and a floor?

a. A pad affects the surrounding surface and a floor element does not.

b. A pad must be placed at a level and a floor can be placed above or below a level.

c. A pad must line up with walls and a floor can also be sketched.

d. A pad cannot be sloped and a floor can be sloped.

5. Why are the topography lines dashed and displayed in red in Figure 1–76? The toposurface has been...

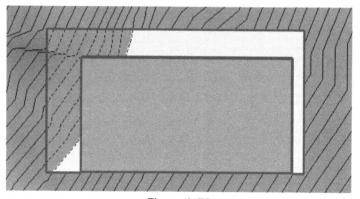

Figure 1–76

a. Edited

b. Graded

c. Demolished

d. Split

6. Which of the following annotations is most helpful when you are modifying the grading of a toposurface?

   a. Label Contours

   b. Spot Elevation

   c. Spot Coordinate

   d. Linear Dimension

7. Which of the following is most likely true about the tree shown on the left in Figure 1–77?

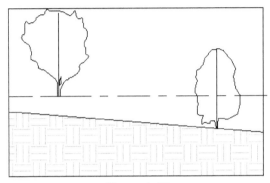

Figure 1–77

   a. It is not a site component.

   b. It is hosted by level.

   c. It has been moved off the surface.

   d. It has been offset above the surface.

8. When you have a site plan linked to a host building project and want to share the coordinates, which of the following should you do?

   a. Acquire the coordinates from the site plan.

   b. Publish the coordinates to the site plan.

Command Summary

Button	Command	Location
Toposurfaces		
	Building Pad	• **Ribbon:** *Massing & Site* tab>Model Site panel
	Edit Boundary	• **Ribbon:** (*select subregion of toposurface*) *Modify	Topography* tab> Subregion panel
	Edit Surface	• **Ribbon:** (*select toposurface*) *Modify	Topography* tab>Surface panel
	Graded Region	• **Ribbon:** *Massing & Site* tab>Modify Site panel
	Merge Surfaces	• **Ribbon:** *Massing & Site* tab>Modify Site panel
	Place Point	• **Ribbon:** *Modify	Edit Surface* tab> Tools panel
	Property Line	• **Ribbon:** *Massing & Site* tab>Modify Site panel
	Select Import Instance	• **Ribbon:** *Modify	Edit Surface* tab> Tools panel>Create from Import drop-down list
	Simplify Surface	• **Ribbon:** *Modify	Edit Surface* tab> Tools panel
	Specify Points File	• **Ribbon:** *Modify	Edit Surface* tab> Tools panel>Create from Import drop-down list
	Split Surface	• **Ribbon:** *Massing & Site* tab>Modify Site panel
	Subregion	• **Ribbon:** *Massing & Site* tab>Modify Site panel
	Toposurface	• **Ribbon:** *Massing & Site* tab>Model Site panel
Other Site Related Tools		
	Label Contours	• **Ribbon:** *Massing & Site* tab>Modify Site panel
	Manage Links	• **Ribbon:** *Manage* tab>Manage Project panel
	Parking Component	• **Ribbon:** *Massing & Site* tab>Model Site panel
	Pick New Host	• **Ribbon:** *Modify	Component* tab> Host panel
	Site Component	• **Ribbon:** *Massing & Site* tab>Model Site panel
	Site Settings	• **Ribbon:** *Massing & Site* tab>Model Site panel title

⊕	**Spot Coordinate**	• **Ribbon:** *Annotate* tab> Dimension panel
⤴	**Spot Elevation**	• **Ribbon:** *Annotate* tab> Dimension panel

Shared Coordinates

⊵	**Acquire Coordinates**	• **Ribbon:** *Manage* tab>Project Location panel>Coordinates drop-down list
🌐	**Location**	• **Ribbon:** *Manage* tab> Project Location panel
⇥	**Publish Coordinates**	• **Ribbon:** *Manage* tab>Project Location panel>Coordinates drop-down list
🔍	**Report Shared Coordinates**	• **Ribbon:** *Manage* tab>Project Location panel>Coordinates drop-down list
1,2	**Specify Coordinates at Point**	• **Ribbon:** *Manage* tab>Project Location panel>Coordinates drop-down list

Structural Tools

Most of the structural work on a project is done by a structural engineer, however architects and designers can learn to use some of the basic structural tools that come with the Autodesk® Revit® software. These tools include all types of structural framing (including columns, beams, and braces), as well as the tools used to create foundations.

Learning Objectives in this Chapter

- Learn the structural basics, including the creation of structural grids and structural columns.
- Create foundations by adding structural walls, wall and slab foundations, and isolated footings.
- Model individual beams and beam systems.
- Add braces.

2.1 Structural Basics

The structural tools in the Autodesk® Revit® software include specialty versions of standard architectural tools (such as columns and walls) as well as tools that are specific to the needs of structural engineers (such as beams and braces). This topic briefly reviews columns and grids (as shown in Figure 2–1), which can speed up the placement of columns.

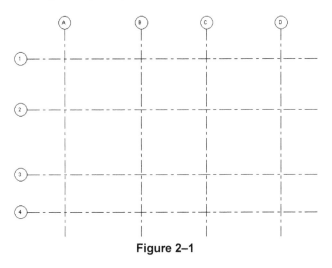

Figure 2–1

Grids Review

Grids indicate the placement of structural column locations. You can add columns to the grid intersections. Each line in a grid is a separate entity and can be placed, moved, and modified individually. The grid type defines the line style and size of the bubble, which is automatically inserted at one end of the line.

How To: Create a Structural Grid

1. In the *Architecture* or *Structure* tab>Datum panel, click ⌗ (Grid).
2. In the Type Selector, select the grid bubble type.
3. In the Draw panel, select one of the Draw tools.
4. In the Options Bar, type a value in the *Offset* field as needed. Draw as many grid lines as required.

- Use temporary dimensions and alignment lines to help position the grids.

- The numbers or letters in the bubbles automatically increment.

- You can use (Copy) and (Array) to help you place grid lines. However, do not make the array as a group, as this could create problems when you modify the grid.

- You can create multi-segment grids, such as that shown in Figure 2–2. When you are in the **Grid** command, in the *Modify | Place Grid* tab>Draw panel, click (Multi-Segment) and use the draw tools to sketch the grid.

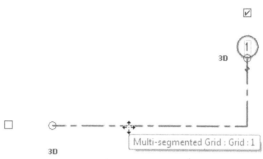

Figure 2–2

- If you have already placed structural columns in the project, they automatically move with any grid that is added later. Select the column and ensure that **Moves with Grids** is selected in the Options Bar.

Adding Structural Columns

The Autodesk Revit software includes two commands for adding columns: one for architectural columns and one for structural columns.

- Architectural columns are typically used as placeholders or decorative elements, as shown in Figure 2–3.

- Structural columns (as shown in Figure 2–4) include more precise information related to industry standards.

If you need the exact sizes of columns, use the more precise structural columns.

Figure 2–3

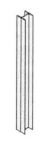

Figure 2–4

- Within structural projects, columns are typically placed from the top down. In architectural projects, they are typically placed from the bottom up. When placing structural columns, specify the **Height** or **Depth** options in the Options Bar before adding the columns.

How To: Add a Vertical Structural Column

1. In the *Architecture* tab>Build panel or *Structure* tab>Structure panel, expand ⎕ (Column) and click ⎕ (Structural Column). The top icon displays the last type used.
2. In the *Modify | Place Structural Column* tab>Placement panel, click ⎕ (Vertical Column).
3. In the Type Selector, select the column type.
4. In the Options Bar, set the options as needed as shown in Figure 2–5.

You can load additional column families from the Library using  (Load Family) in the Mode panel.

Figure 2–5

- Select **Rotate after placement** or press the <Spacebar> to toggle through the rotation options.
- Set the **Height** or **Depth** and the **Level** or **Unconnected** height from the drop-down lists. If you select **Unconnected**, you can also type a distance.

5. In the *Modify | Place Structural Column* tab>Tag panel, click ⌐① (Tag on Placement) to add tags.
6. Place the column. It can be placed as a free instance or can snap to grid lines and walls. You can also place multiple instances:

- Click ⊶ (At Grids) and select the grids with the intersections at which you want the columns to be placed.

- Click ⬚ (At Columns) and select existing architectural columns to place structural columns within the existing columns, as shown in Figure 2–6.

Figure 2–6

- Click ✓ (Finish) to complete either of the multiple options.

7. Continue placing columns as needed.

- You can also use ⟲ (Copy) and ⊞ (Array) to speed up column placement.

Hint: Slanted Columns

Slanted columns can be added in a plan, elevation, section, or 3D view, as shown in Figure 2–7.

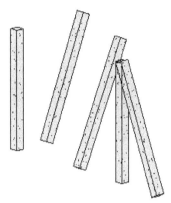

Figure 2–7

The most precise way to use this command is as follows:

1. Start the **Structural Column** command.
2. In the *Modify | Place Structural Column* tab>Placement panel, click ∅ (Slanted Column).
3. In the Options bar, select **3D Snapping** and select points for the two ends.

Loading Structural Column Sizes

Hundreds of standard-sized columns are available in the Autodesk Revit Library. The columns are divided into folders for Concrete, Light Gauge Steel, Precast Concrete, Steel, and Wood, as shown in Figure 2–8.

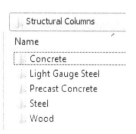

Figure 2–8

- As there are many different sizes for each type of column, you may need to filter the column types to find the one you need.

How To: Select and Load Specific Column Types

1. In the *Modify | Place Structural Column* tab>Mode panel, click 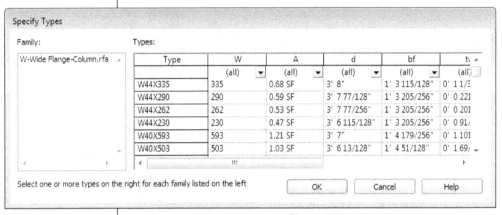 (Load Family).
2. In the Load Family dialog box, select a column type and click **Open**.
3. In the Specify Types dialog box (shown in Figure 2–9), select the column types you want to load and click **OK**.

Specify Types

Family:

	Types:				
W-Wide Flange-Column.rfa	Type	W	A	d	bf	t\
		(all)	(all)	(all)	(all)	(all)
	W44X335	335	0.68 SF	3' 8"	1' 3 115/128"	0' 1 1/:
	W44X290	290	0.59 SF	3' 7 77/128"	1' 3 205/256"	0' 0 22]
	W44X262	262	0.53 SF	3' 7 77/256"	1' 3 205/256"	0' 0 20]
	W44X230	230	0.47 SF	3' 6 115/128"	1' 3 205/256"	0' 0 91/
	W40X593	593	1.21 SF	3' 7"	1' 4 179/256"	0' 1 10]
	W40X503	503	1.03 SF	3' 6 13/128"	1' 4 51/128"	0' 1 69/

Select one or more types on the right for each family listed on the left

[OK] [Cancel] [Help]

Figure 2–9

- Use the drop-down lists at the top of each column to filter your search for the required shapes and sizes. This enables you to load only the columns that you want to use.

Practice 2a

Structural Basics

Estimated time for completion: 20 minutes

Practice Objectives

- Draw a structural grid.
- Load and add several different types of structural columns.

In this practice you will create a grid and add various columns, as shown in Figure 2–10. The column sizes are exaggerated to indicate the locations.

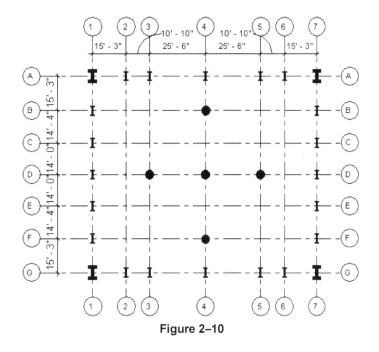

Figure 2–10

Task 1 - Add structural grids.

1. Start a new project based on the default architectural template. Save the project in the practice files folder as **Warehouse.rvt**.

2. In the *Architecture* or *Structure* tab>Datum panel, click
   (Grid) and draw the grid lines shown in Figure 2–10.

   - The vertical grids are placed at 15'-3, 10'-10", 25'-6", 25'-6", 10'-10", and 15'-3".
   - The horizontal grids are placed at 15'-3", 14'-4", 14'-0", 14'-0", 14'-4", and 15'-3".

3. To have the grid bubbles display at both ends, select one of the grid lines and edit the type. In the Type Properties dialog box, select **Plan View Symbols End 1** and **Plan View Symbols End 2**.

4. Save the project.

Task 2 - Add structural columns.

1. In the *Architecture* tab>Build panel, expand ⬚ (Column) and select ⬚ (Structural Column). Alternatively, in the *Structure* tab>Structure panel, click ⬚ (Column).

2. In the *Modify | Place Structural Column* tab>Mode panel, click ⬚ (Load Family).

3. In the Load family dialog box, navigate to the *Structural Columns>Steel* folder and select **W-Wide Flange-Column.rfa**. Click **Open**.

4. In the Specify Types dialog box, select the **W8x31** and **W8x28** column types, and then click **OK**.

5. If required, in the Family Already Exists dialog box, select the **Override the existing version and its parameter values** option to import the new Wide Flange sizes.

6. Repeat the Load Family command and load the steel column **Pipe-Column: Pipe6STD**.

7. Add the structural columns that are listed in the table and shown in Figure 2–10.

Four (4) exterior corners	W-Wide Flange-Column: W8x31
Other exterior grid intersections	W-Wide Flange-Column: W8x28
Five interior locations	Pipe-Column: Pipe6STD

8. Save the project.

2.2 Creating Foundations

Foundations can include structural walls, foundations (walls, slabs, and isolated), and retaining walls, as shown in Figure 2–11.

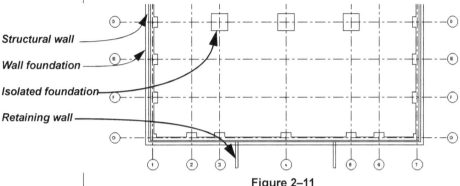

Structural wall

Wall foundation

Isolated foundation

Retaining wall

Figure 2–11

Adding Structural Walls

Wall types can function as interior, exterior, retaining, or foundation walls. Examples of each of these are supplied with the templates in the software and you can also create custom wall types. Any type can be a structural bearing wall—one that supports a weight other than its own.

- To access structural walls, in the *Architecture* tab>Build panel, expand (Wall) and click (Wall: Structural). Alternatively, in the *Structural* tab>Structure panel, click. (Wall: Structural).

- Structural walls are typically drawn from the top down. For this reason, the **Wall: Structural** command defaults to *Depth* rather than *Height*. Any change to this selection remains as long as you are in the same session of Autodesk Revit.

Structural walls are created in the same manner as standard walls.

- When you create a structural wall, the *Structural Usage* is set to **Bearing** (as shown in Figure 2–12), while the standard **Walls** command sets it to **Non-bearing**. You can change the usage when the wall is in the project.

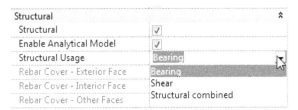

Figure 2–12

Structural Usage Options

Non-bearing	Walls are not designed to support any load other than their own weight.
Bearing	Walls support a vertical load and their own weight.
Shear	Walls support loads coming in laterally, such as a retaining wall.
Structural combined	Walls serve more than one purpose.

- Structural walls can be drawn in plan and 3D views.

- You can change the profile of a structural wall in a 3D or elevation view. Select a wall. In the *Modify | Walls* tab>Mode panel, click (Edit Profile) and modify the profile of the wall as shown in Figure 2–13. If footings are associated with the wall, the footings are also modified.

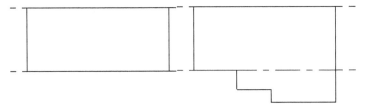

Figure 2–13

Wall Foundations

You can apply wall foundation (footings) under any structural wall, as shown in Figure 2–14. They are attached to the bottom of the wall, and therefore a wall must be in place in order to add them.

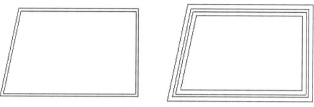

Figure 2–14

- To display the footing in a floor plan view, set the *View Depth* in the View Range dialog box to display the level below. You can also create a foundation level and set it as an underlay in the plan view.

How To: Add Wall Foundations

1. In the *Structure* tab>Foundation panel, click 🔲 (Wall).
2. Select each wall that you want the footing to be under.
   - Press <Tab> to highlight all connected walls before selecting a wall.
   - To use a window or crossing selection, in the *Modify | Place Wall Foundation* tab> Multiple panel click

     🔲 (Select Multiple). Click ✓ (Finish) when all of the walls you want are selected.

- Wall Foundations are system families. Two types come with the templates that are included with the Autodesk Revit software (as shown in Figure 2–15), and you can create

  custom types using 🔲 (Edit Type).

Figure 2–15

- You can tag and schedule information about wall foundations.

- Wall foundations move with the associated walls.

Hint: Editing Foundation Types

New sizes for walls and isolated structural foundations can be created by adding types to an existing system family. For example, edit the type of the default Bearing Footing, duplicate the existing type, and then modify the dimensions, as shown in Figure 2–16.

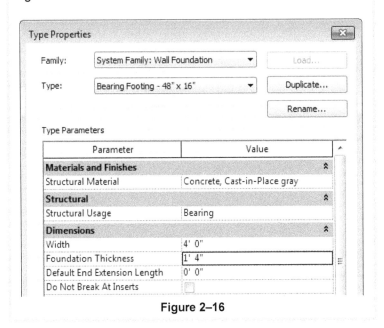

Figure 2–16

Individual Footings and Pile Caps

You can also add components for footings and pile caps to a foundation plan. The Autodesk Revit software includes a rectangular footing (as shown in Figure 2–17), and several styles of pile caps in the Revit Library in the *Structural Foundations* folder.

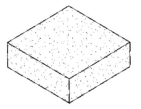

Figure 2–17

How To: Add Isolated Footings

1. In the *Structure* tab>Foundation panel, click ⬇ (Isolated).
   - If a Structural Foundation family has not been loaded, an alert box opens. Click **Yes** to load a family.
2. In the Type Selector, select the type that you want to use.
3. Click to place the footing.

- To place multiple isolated footings, you can use ⬚ (At Grids) or ⬚ (At Columns).

- The footing component is automatically placed in the drawing with the top of the footing at the current level. Therefore, the footing does not display in the current level view unless you use View Properties to set the **View Depth** or **Underlay** options to be visible.

- Foundation Walls and Isolated footings clean up if they are the same type of material as shown in Figure 2–18.

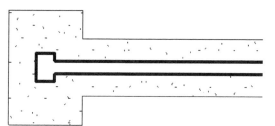

Figure 2–18

- You can create custom footing and pile cap sizes using ⬚ (Edit Type).

Foundation Slabs and Structural Floors

Some buildings include structural elements called *slab on grade*. These floor areas, also called foundation slabs, are structural elements and do not require additional support. For example, the base of the elevator shaft in Figure 2–19 is a foundation slab.

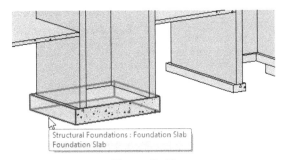

Structural Foundations : Foundation Slab
Foundation Slab

Figure 2–19

Three types of floor-like elements are used in the Autodesk Revit software: Floors, Structural Floors, and Foundation Slabs. They are all created using the same methods.

- By default, the top of the floor matches the height of the level.

How To: Draw Slabs

1. Proceed as per the table below:

To draw a...	Then...
Foundation slab	In the *Structure* tab>Foundation panel, click ⬭ (Structural Foundation: Slab).
Structural floor	In the *Architecture* tab>Build panel or *Structure* tab> Structure panel, expand ⬭ (Floor) and click ⌒ (Structural Floor)

2. In the *Modify | Create Floor Boundary* tab>Draw panel, click
    ⅃ (Boundary Line).

    - Use the Draw tools (such as ⟋ (Line) or ⚟ (Pick Lines)), when the slab is not defined by walls or a structure and is free-floating.

    - Use 🗔 (Pick Walls) when walls define the perimeter.

    - Use 🗔 (Pick Supports) and select structural walls or beams when the slab is supported by beams.

3. Click ⬚ (Span Direction) to modify the direction for floor spans. It comes in automatically when you place the first boundary line.

4. ⟨⟩ (Flip) switches the inside/outside status of the boundary location if you have selected a wall, as shown in Figure 2–20.

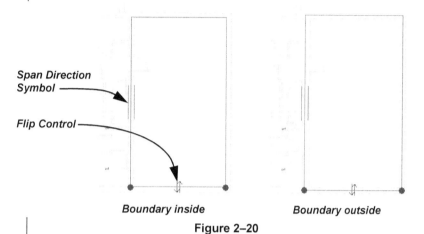

Span Direction Symbol

Flip Control

Boundary inside   **Boundary outside**

Figure 2–20

5. In the *Modify | Create Floor Boundary* tab>Mode panel, click ✓ (Finish Edit Mode).

Practice 2b

Create Foundations

Practice Objectives

- Add walls and retaining walls.
- Add footings under walls and columns.

Estimated time for completion: 10 minutes

In this practice you will add standard walls and retaining walls. You will then load a footing, create new footing sizes, and add footings to the project, as shown in Figure 2–21.

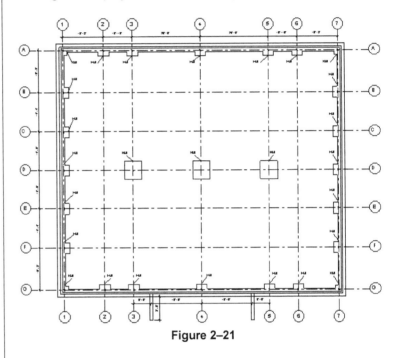

Figure 2–21

Task 1 - Add Walls and Retaining Walls.

1. In the practice files folder, open the project **Warehouse-Foundation.rvt**.

2. Duplicate the **Floor Plans: Level 1** view and rename it as **Foundation Plan**.

3. In Properties, edit the *View Range* and set the *Primary Range: Bottom Offset* and *View Depth: Level Offset* to (negative) **–2-0"** so that the footings display when you add them.

4. In the *Architecture* tab>Build panel, click  (Wall).

5. In the Type Selector, select **Basic Wall: Generic - 8"
Masonry** with the *Height* set to **Unconnected: 20'-0"**.

6. Draw a wall **1'-1"** outside the grid line around the outside the
building, as shown in Figure 2–22.

Figure 2–22

7. In the *Structure* tab>Structure panel, expand  (Wall) and

click (Wall: Structural). Add two walls at the front of the
building as shown in Figure 2–23. Use the type **Basic Wall:
Retaining 12" Concrete** with the *Height* set to **4'-0"**.

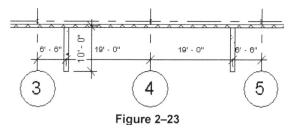

Figure 2–23

Task 2 - Add Footings.

1. In the *Structure* tab>Foundation panel, click (Wall). In the
Type Selector, select **Wall Foundation: Bearing Footing-
36"x12"** and add a footing around all of the exterior walls, as
shown in Figure 2–24.

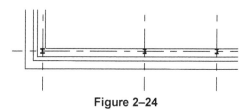

Figure 2–24

2. In the *Structure* tab>Foundation panel, click (Isolated).
Load the family **Footing – Rectangular.rfa** from the Library
(in the Structural>*Foundations* folder).

3. In Properties, click 🔲 (Edit Type) and create new footing types with the following sizes:

Name and Type Mark	Footing Size
F3.0	3'-0" x 3'-0" x 1'-0"
F4.0	4'-0" x 4'-0" x 1'-0"
F6.5	6'-6" x 6'-6" x 1'-0"

4. Add the footings as shown in the foundation plan in Figure 2–25 and in the Footing information in Step 3.

If you have time, add dimensions and tags to the footings. The tags for foundation elements that come with the software display the type name.

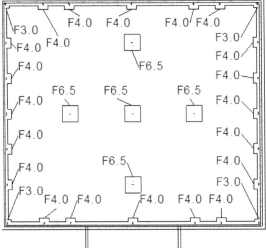

Figure 2–25

The footings automatically clean up with the wall foundations, as shown in Figure 2–26.

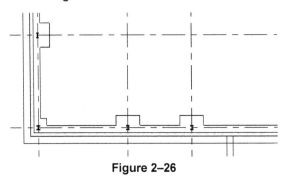

Figure 2–26

5. Save the project.

2.3 Modeling Structural Framing

The Autodesk® Revit® software enables you to frame a building with wood, concrete, and steel framing and bracing, such as the steel example shown in Figure 2–27. You can add individual beams, as well as beam systems and bracing elements.

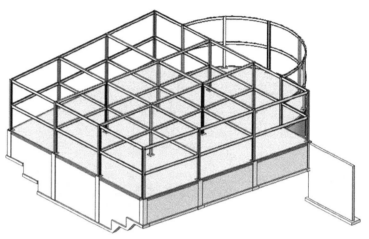

Figure 2–27

- Framing types include: **Concrete**, **Light Gauge Steel**, **Precast Concrete**, **Steel**, and **Wood**.

- In views set to a **Coarse** detail level, the software assigns a lineweight to the structural members based on their structural usage. For example, a Girder displays in a heavier lineweight than a Joist, while a Purlin displays with a dashed line. as shown in Figure 2–28.

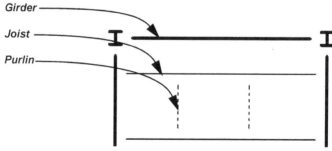

Figure 2–28

- When modeling beams, the View Range for Floor Plans needs to be set below the current level. For example, set the *Bottom Offset* to (negative) **-4'-0''** and the *View Depth Level* to (negative) **-6-0''** to match standard Structural Plan views.

How To: Add Beams

1. In the *Structure* tab>Structure panel, click ✏️ (Beam).
2. In the Type Selector, select a beam type.
3. In the Options Bar, specify the options, as shown in Figure 2–29 and described below.

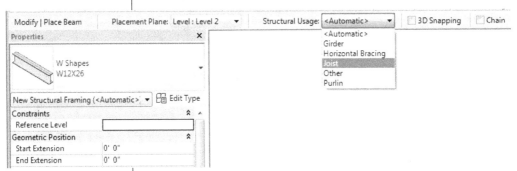

Figure 2–29

- *Placement Plane:* Defaults to the current level if you are in a plan view but can be modified to other levels.
- *Structural Usage:* Select a type (as shown in Figure 2–29), or accept the default of **<Automatic>**.
- **3D Snapping:** Select this if you want to draw a beam from one point to another at different heights.
- **Chain:** Select this if you want to draw a series of beams in a row. To stay in the command and start another chain, press <Esc> once.
4. For automatic tagging, in the *Modify | Place Beam* tab>Tag panel, click 🏷️ (Tag on Placement).
5. In the *Modify | Place Beam* tab>Draw panel, use the Draw tools to draw the beams.

How To: Add Multiple Beams on Grid Lines

1. Start the Beam command and specify the type and other options, as outlined above.

2. In the *Modify | Place Beam* tab>Multiple panel, click ⚏ (On Grids).

3. Select the grids where you want to locate the beams. A beam is placed between each grid intersection, as shown in Figure 2–30. Hold <Ctrl> to select more than one grid, or use a pick and drag window to select multiple grids at one time.

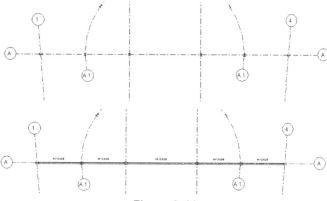

Figure 2–30

4. In the *Modify | Place Beam>On Grid Line* tab>Multiple panel, click ✓ (Finish).

• Sometimes this can be the quickest way to add beams. If you need to use various sizes of beams, when you are finished, select those beams and make any changes in the Type Selector.

Beam Systems

Beam Systems are layouts of parallel beams placed between other beams, as shown in Figure 2–31. Typically used in joist layouts, beam systems can be set up to use either a fixed distance or number of beams. You can create beam systems automatically, but the automatic method might not find the correct reference beams or walls, or you might want to include an opening within the system. In these cases, you can also create a sketch for your beam system.

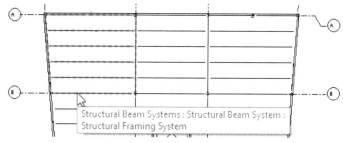

Figure 2–31

How To: Add Automatic Beam Systems

1. In the *Structure* tab>Structure panel, click ▥ (Beam System) or type **BS**.
2. The *Modify | Place Structural Beam System* tab>Beam System panel, click ▥ (Automatic Beam System).
   - To automatically label the Beam Systems as they are placed, in the Tag panel, click ⌂ (Tag on Placement) and in the Options Bar, set the *Tag Style:* to **Framing**, which tags each individual member, or **System** which places one tag for the entire framing system) as shown in Figure 2–32.

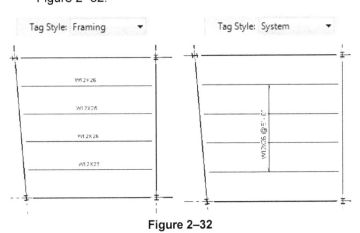

Figure 2–32

3. In the Options Bar (shown in Figure 2–33), set the *Beam Type*, *Justification*, and *Layout Rule*.

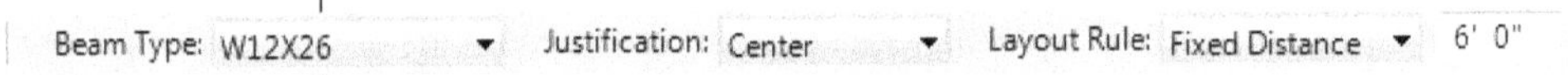

Beam Type: W12X26 ▼   Justification: Center ▼   Layout Rule: Fixed Distance ▼   6' 0"

Figure 2–33

   - The *Layout Rules* include: **Clear Spacing**, **Fixed Distance**, **Fixed Number**, and **Maximum Spacing**. Set the required distance or number.
   - Make changes in Properties or in the Options Bar as needed to establish the required beam system.

4. Move the cursor over an existing beam until the guide lines display in the correct area and direction, as shown vertically and horizontally in Figure 2–34.

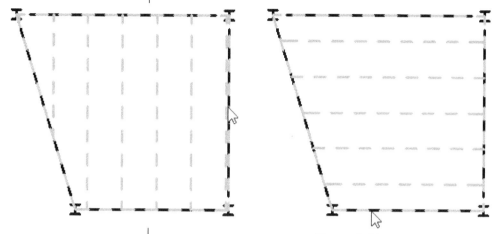

Figure 2–34

5. Select the existing beam to place the system.
6. Repeat this step in other bays as required.

- The Beam System is one uniform group. You can change beam's type, spacing, and elevation in Properties or in the Options Bar.

- If a grid line is moved, the beams automatically space themselves. If the bay increases beyond the minimum spacing, a beam is added. If the bay shrinks below the allowable spacing, a beam is removed.

- If you need to change the system to individual beams, in the *Modify | Structural Beam Systems* tab>Beam System panel, click (Remove Beam System). The individual beams remain but are no longer grouped together.

How To: Sketch a Beam System

1. In the *Structure* tab>Structure panel, click (Beam System).
2. In the *Modify | Place Structural Beam System* tab>Beam System panel, click (Sketch Beam System).

3. In the *Modify | Create Beam System Boundary* tab>Draw panel, click 🔳 (Pick Supports) or use one of the other drawing tools.

4. In the Draw panel, click ⁞⁞⁞ (Beam Direction) and select one of the sketch lines that runs as you want the system to run, as shown on the top horizontal beam in Figure 2–35.

Figure 2–35

5. Clean up all of the corners so that there are no overlaps or gaps.
6. In the *Modify | Create Beam System Boundary* tab>Mode panel, click ✓ (Finish Edit Mode).
7. Make changes in Properties or in the Options Bar as needed to establish the required beam system.

- To include an opening in a beam system, draw another opening inside the original sketched boundary.

Adding Bracing

Braces automatically attach to other structural elements, such as beams, columns, and walls. They recognize typical snap points such as the end point of a column and the middle of a beam, as shown in Figure 2–36.

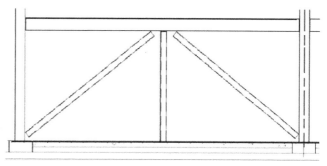

Figure 2–36

- Bracing can be added in plan view or in a framing elevation view. Framing elevations are similar to interior elevations. The elevation marker is placed between two columns and limits the scope of the elevation to that distance, as shown in Figure 2–37.

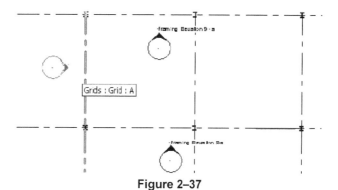

Figure 2–37

How To: Create a Framing Elevation

1. Open a floor plan view that includes grid lines.

2. In the *View* tab>Create panel, expand ⌂ (Elevation) and click ⌂ (Framing Elevation).

3. Hover the cursor over the grid line that you want to display in elevation. A preview of the elevation marker displays.

4. Click to set the marker on one side of the line. The arrow automatically points toward the grid line.

5. The new elevation is listed in the Project Browser in the *Interior Elevations* area, as shown in Figure 2–38. You can rename it as needed.

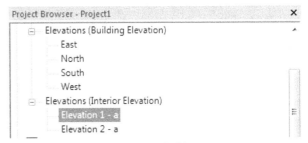

Figure 2–38

6. Open the new elevation. By default, it only displays one bay of the grid.

• Framing elevations display all of the levels by default, but you can resize the crop region as needed. Open the elevation view and add braces and other detail objects.

How To: Add Bracing

1. Create and open a framing elevation.

2. In the *Structure* tab>Structure panel, click ⊠ (Brace).
3. In the Type Selector, select a brace type.
4. Pick two points for the end points of the brace. Work from the centerline of all of framing members so that the analytical line extends into the adjacent framing, even though the graphical member stops at the edge of the column or beam, as shown in Figure 2–39.

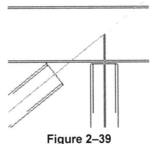

Figure 2–39

Practice 2c

Model Structural Framing

Estimated time for completion: 10 minutes

Practice Objectives

- Create a structural framing plan and a framing elevation.
- Add beams and braces

In this practice you will add beams to a roof framing plan, as shown in Figure 2–40, create a framing elevation, and add braces.

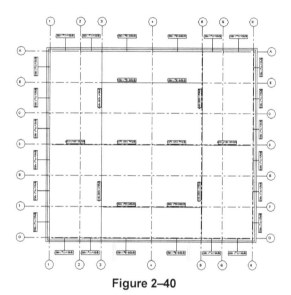

Figure 2–40

Task 1 - Create a structural framing plan and add beams.

1. In the practice files folder, open the project **Warehouse-Framing.rvt**.

2. In the Project Browser, right-click on the Floor Plans: **Level 2** view and select **Duplicate View>Duplicate**. Rename it **Roof-Framing Plan**.

3. In Properties, open the View Range dialog box and set the *Primary Range Bottom* to (negative) **-4'-0"** and *View Depth Level* to (negative) **-6'-0"**.

4. In the *Annotate* tab>Tag panel, expand the title and click 🔄 (Loaded Tags and Symbols). In the Loaded Tags and Symbols dialog box, click **Load Family...**.

5. In the Library's *Annotations>Structural* folder, load **Structural Framing Tag.rfa** and click **OK** twice.

6. In the *Insert* tab>Load from Library panel, click 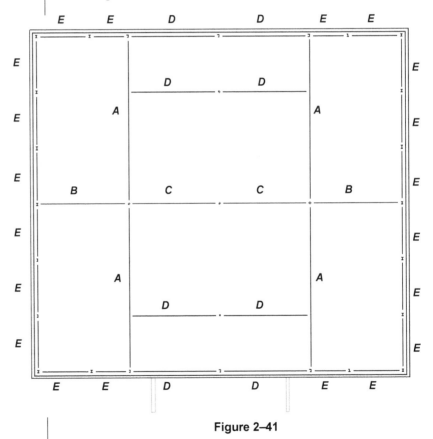 (Load Family. In the *Structural Framing>Steel* folder, open the family **W-Wide Flange.rfa**. In the Specify Types dialog box, select the following types, overriding any existing versions: when prompted: (The letters refer to the next step in the practice.)

- **W24 x 68 (A)**
- **W21 x 48 (B)**
- **W18 x 40 (C)**
- **W16 x 26 (D)**
- **W14 x 22 (E)**

Hold down <Ctrl> to select multiple sizes in the Specify Types dialog box.

7. Add the beams as shown in Figure 2–41, using the letters listed in Step 6. They are symmetrical on either side of the building. You can use a variety of techniques to insert them, including sketching one or a chain of beams, or selecting grids to place the beam. In the Option Bar, set *Structural Usage* to be **<Automatic>**.

The beams are shown without the grids for clarity.

Figure 2–41

Task 2 - Create a framing elevation and add braces.

1. Add a framing elevation along column line G between grid lines 3 and 4 on the exterior wall, as shown in Figure 2–42.

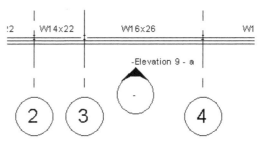

Figure 2–42

2. Switch to the new framing elevation. The elevation number might vary.

3. Adjust the elevation boundaries to display the columns, beams, and footings.

4. Add the brace **C-Channel C12 x 20.7** between the columns shown in Figure 2–43. You need to load it from the Library (*Structural Framing>Steel>***C-Channel.rfa**).

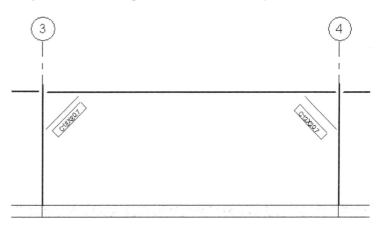

Figure 2–43

5. Save the project.

Chapter Review Questions

1. In which type of view would you place structural braces?

   a. Framing Plans

   b. Framing Elevations

   c. Structural Plans

   d. Structural Elevations

2. Which of the following processes best describes how you add wall foundations, as shown in Figure 2–44?

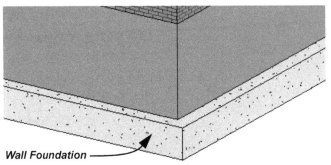

Wall Foundation

Figure 2–44

   a. Use draw tools and trace the existing walls.

   b. Use Sketch Mode and draw new walls.

   c. Select the existing walls.

   d. Add a foundation component under the existing walls.

3. Which element is the host for an isolated footing?

   a. Column

   b. Wall

   c. Slab

   d. Floor

4. What is the difference between a structural floor and an architectural floor?

   a. Structural floors include analytical properties while architectural floors do not.

   b. Structural floors are offset down from the current level while architectural floors are drawn at the current level.

   c. Structural floors cannot include multiple slopes while architectural floors can.

   d. Structural floors have a direction while architectural floors do not.

5. When placing a beam, such as that shown in Figure 2–45, which of the following is NOT an option?

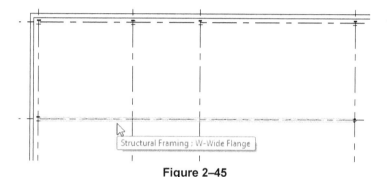

Figure 2–45

   a. **Structural Usage**

   b. **Placement Plane**

   c. **3D Snapping**

   d. **At Columns**

6. Which of the following describes a Beam System?

   a. Parallel beams grouped together after they are placed.

   b. Parallel beams placed at the same time.

   c. All beams within a bay are grouped together after they are placed.

   d. All beams within a bay that are placed at the same time.

7. Columns must be placed at structural grid intersections as shown in Figure 2–46.

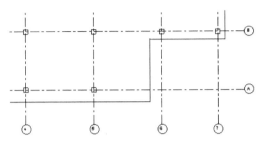

Figure 2–46

a. True

b. False

Command Summary

Button	Command	Location
Basics		
	Grid	• **Ribbon:** *Architecture* or *Structure* tab>Datum panel
	Structural Column	• **Ribbon:** *Architecture* tab>Build panel or *Structure* tab>Structure panel> expand Column
	Structural Column: At Columns	• **Ribbon:** *Modify | Place Structural Column* tab>Multiple panel
	Structural Column: At Grids	• **Ribbon:** *Modify | Place Structural Column* tab>Multiple panel
	Structural Column: Slanted Column	• **Ribbon:** *Modify | Place Structural Column* tab>Placement panel
	Structural Column: Vertical Column	• **Ribbon:** *Modify | Place Structural Column* tab>Placement panel
	Structural Wall	• **Ribbon:** *Architecture* tab>Build panel or *Structure* tab>Structure panel> expand Wall
Foundations		
	(Foundation) Slab	• **Ribbon:** *Structure* tab>Foundation panel>expand Slab
	Isolated (Foundation)	• **Ribbon:** *Structure* tab>Foundation panel
	Wall (Foundation)	• **Ribbon:** *Structure* tab>Foundation panel
Structural Framing		
	Beam	• **Ribbon:** *Structure* tab>Structure panel
	Beam System	• **Ribbon:** *Structure* tab>Structure panel
	Brace	• **Ribbon:** *Structure* tab>Structure panel
	Framing Elevation	• **Ribbon:** *View* tab>Create panel> expand Elevation

Appendix

A

Autodesk Revit Architecture Certification Exam Objectives

The following table will help you to locate the exam objectives within the chapters of the Autodesk® Revit® student guides to help you prepare for the Autodesk Revit Architecture Certified Professional exam.

Exam Topic	Exam Objective	Training Guide	Chapter & Section(s)
Collaboration	Copy and monitor elements in a linked file	• Revit Collaboration Tools	• 2.3
	Use worksharing	• Revit Collaboration Tools	• 4.1 to 4.3
	Import DWG and image files	• Revit Architecture Fundamentals	• 3.4
		• Revit Collaboration Tools	• 3.1 to 3.3
	Use Worksharing Visualization	• Revit Collaboration Tools	• 4.4
	Assess review warnings in Revit	• Revit Architecture Fundamentals	• 12.1
Documentation	Create and modify filled regions	• Revit Architecture Fundamentals	• 16.3
	Place detail components and repeating details	• Revit Architecture Fundamentals	• 16.2
	Tag elements (doors, windows, etc.) by category	• Revit Architecture Fundamentals	• 15.1
	Use dimension strings	• Revit Architecture Fundamentals	• 14.1
	Set the colors used in a color scheme legend	• Revit Architecture: Conceptual Design and Visualization	• 2.3
	Work with phases	• Revit Collaboration Tools	• 1.1

Exam Topic	Exam Objective	Training Guide	Chapter & Section(s)
Elements and Families	Change elements within a curtain wall (grids, panels, mullions	• Revit Architecture Fundamentals	• 6.2 to 6.4
	Create compound walls	• Revit BIM Management	• 3.1
	Create a stacked wall	• Revit BIM Management	• 3.3
	Differentiate system and component families	• Revit BIM Management	• 3.1 • 4.1
	Work with family parameters	• Revit BIM Management	• 4.2
	Create a new family type	• Revit Architecture Fundamentals	• 5.3
		• Revit BIM Management	• 4.4
	Use family creation procedures	• Revit BIM Management	• 4.1 to 4.4
Modeling	Create a building pad	• Revit Architecture: Site and Structure	• 1.2
	Define floor for a mass	• Revit Architecture: Conceptual Design and Visualization	• 1.7
	Create a stair with a landing	• Revit Architecture Fundamentals	• 12.1
	Create elements such as floors, ceilings, or roofs	• Revit Architecture Fundamentals	• 9.1 • 10.1 • 11.2 & 11.4
	Generate a toposurface	• Revit Architecture: Site and Structure	• 1.1
	Model railings	• Revit Architecture Fundamentals	• 12.3
	Edit a model element's material (door, window, furniture)	• Revit Architecture Fundamentals	• 5.3 • B.4
	Change a generic floor / ceiling / roof to a specific type	• Revit Architecture Fundamentals	• 9.1 • 10.1 • 11.2
	Attach walls to a roof or ceiling	• Revit Architecture Fundamentals	• 11.2
	Edit room-aware families	• Revit BIM Management	• 5.1

Exam Topic	Exam Objective	Training Guide	Chapter & Section(s)
Views	Define element properties in a schedule	• Revit Architecture Fundamentals	• 15.3
	Control visibility	• Revit Architecture Fundamentals	• 7.1
	Use levels	• Revit Architecture Fundamentals	• 3.1
	Create a duplicate view for a plan, section, elevation, drafting view, etc.	• Revit Architecture Fundamentals	• 7.2
	Create and manage legends	• Revit Architecture Fundamentals	• 14.4
	Manage view position on sheets	• Revit Architecture Fundamentals	• 13.2
	Organize and sort items in a schedule	• Revit Architecture Fundamentals	• B.10
		• Revit BIM Management	• 2.2

Index

www.ingramcontent.com/pod-product-compliance
Lightning Source LLC
LaVergne TN
LVHW080101070326
832902LV00014B/2356